Women Belong in Leadership

Let Critics Keep Silent

Women Belong in Leadership

Let Critics Keep Silent

Kay Ramnarine

WIPF & STOCK · Eugene, Oregon

WOMEN BELONG IN LEADERSHIP: LET CRITICS KEEP SILENT

Wipf & Stock Publishers
199 W. 8th Ave., Suite 3
Eugene, OR 97401

ISBN 13: 978-1-55635-576-9

Manufactured in the U.S.A.

Acknowledgments

This book could not have been possible without the assistance and support of several individuals. I sincerely thank each one of them for their invaluable contribution.

I thank Dr. Kenneth Ragoonath, President of the Open Bible Institute of Theology of Trinidad & Tobago, and Dr. Dale W. Kietzman and Dr. James K. Krames of the Newport University, U.S.A. for making this book a reality. I also thank Dr. Ruth Kietzman for her valuable comments and helpful guidelines regarding the first draft.

I express my sincerest gratitude to my pastor and mentor, Rev Winston Ballosingh, for affording me the opportunities to grow and develop in ministerial leadership. I also thank his wife, Rev Selma Ballosingh for her support and prayers.

I specially thank my sister, Nita, for proof-reading and moral support throughout the exercise.

Many thanks to Tricia de Gannes for her typing services and general support at crucial times. Tricia was a reliable source when computer glitches were encountered; I also thank Bert Williams and Beverly Reid in this regard.

I also express heartfelt appreciation to the ministers and leaders of the Central Missions Foundation churches at Penal and Princes Town for their faithful and consistent assistance with pastoral and administrative duties and for their support in the church building projects at both locations. Also, special thanks to Patricia de Gannes and the faculty and staff of the Ministerial Training Institute for holding the reigns particularly during the last few months to completion of the manuscript.

I am greatly indebted to Dr. James K. Krames for his editorial skill in making the manuscript more presentable and readable.

Finally, I express my gratitude to the many scholars and writers who helped me to interpret the relevant "difficult" Bible passages and who provided excellent material on the subject. To this end I acknowledge Ruth A.Tucker & Walter Liefeld; Loren Cunningham & David Joel Hamilton; and John Temple Bristow.

July 2007
Kay Ramnarine

Contents

Abbreviations

ESV	English Standard Version
KJV	King James Version, 1990
NIV	New International Version, 1996
NJKV	New King James Version, 1985

Foreword

A Woman's Place in the Church: A Biblical View
by Dale W. Kietzman, PhD

Kay Ramnarine has tackled a thorny subject, but it is one in which she is an active player. She can, and does, argue from personal experience, but she also has addressed the most common arguments against women in the pulpit with sound Biblical interpretation.

The work reflects throughout Ramnarine's own personal experience as a Christian worker who eventually is placed in the role of Senior Pastor, in which role she has demonstrated successfully her spiritual gifting, as well as her charismatic personality. So this study is neither impersonal nor theoretical but a well argued, impassioned plea for understanding for all women in her same situation.

The chapters on tradition and culture are much to the point, because they chart the way in which opposition to women in ministry has developed. This background is essential to bring those of us who might be skeptical of the premise to see the logic of the arguments put forward to support the role that women have taken in the Church, and which, it seems, they must take when faced by the inaction of men.

Ramnarine closes with a seemingly defiant "We'll rather obey God", but in actuality she is attempting to open doors for women to demonstrate their leadership gifts within their fellowship circles. May God bless them in their endeavors!

Dale W. Kietzman, PhD
Executive Vice-President
William Carey International University

PART ONE
Introduction

Introduction

In every century, and especially today's, no issue has divided the organized church as that dealing with the nature and scope of leadership roles open to women.

Swirling about the debate are such questions as the ordination of women, and especially their call to executive pastoral positions. In the matrix of this controversial issue are these additional questions:

- Is the pulpit intended for female preachers?
- Is it biblical for women to teach men?
- Can a woman serve as a bishop, senior pastor, elder or deacon?

At every turn the legitimacy of women to perform vocational ministries (pastoring, preaching, and governing) that have been traditionally reserved for men is being challenged.

Of course, there is no debate about some roles for women. They are welcome to attend all church services. They are welcome to keep the sanctuary clean and presentable. They are welcome as rain to serve in the communion service, preparing the bread and wine. In addition, one must not forget the secretarial duties—who can serve in this capacity like a member of the 'fairer sex'? In fact, among 99% of all roles and offices in the local church, they are welcome to participate, and all would agree, are much needed.

How many forests of trees have been chopped down to produce the paper for the many books, articles and position papers published to deal with the hot debate regarding women in senior pastoral positions exercising weekly pulpit ministries in local congregations. No one is neutral on this issue.

However, while many church leaders and organizations, globally, are embracing views that are more progressive in giving women in ministry the freedom to fulfill any and every call of God on their lives, many remain adamant that women should "…keep silent in the church."

What is it that has brought these limits on godly women? Research shows that the main contributing factors are tradition, culture, and Scripture. These weapons are wielded by both sides of this debate to support their case in support or opposition to restricting and suppressing the call of women to higher leadership.

This book will examine, from several perspectives, this issue, and investigate the legitimacy of the factors listed above. We shall carefully analyze the relevant difficult Scriptures often quoted and used to prohibit women's participation in higher leadership.

This paper will also address the functions of women in Bible days, both in the Old and New Testaments as well as address the contribution women have made over the past decades, in pioneering church denominations, and their invaluable service in world missions.

You will discover a strong case for the true place of women in the church—leading!

This book is divided into four main parts.

Part One deals with the personal story of my ministry. It is important that you understand what has happened to me in the course of serving the Lord during the last two decades of ministry. Otherwise, you will not have a "context" from which to understand the issues that I address.

Therefore, I begin with the story of my own personal experience. It will provide you a context from which to understand the issues I choose to address. It will also help you to understand the reasoning behind the opinions I have formed and the views that I take concerning each issue addressed.

Part Two focuses on the Biblical Arguments that have been leveled at me. I will first describe for you the cultural and traditional basis for the thinking that has opposed my ministry. Then, in four subsequent chapters I will focus on one of the four primary Biblical arguments that my Detractors have used in attempting to persuade me to leave the calling I have obeyed for so long.

Part Three examines those women that have played strategically important roles throughout church history. Beginning with Eve and tracing women in each major era, this section will demonstrate that the Lord, the Apostles, and historical circumstances have turned to women to support the leadership roles of men during times within the Church's most critical moments of transition and change.

In Part Four, we shall pull our ideas together in a summary discussion. It makes my argument better than I have ever presented when personally confronted by my Detractors.

So, if you have stood in my shoes, faced similar Detractors, or are considering ministry but being buffeted by people who oppose the Lord's leading because you are a woman, welcome to the debate.

I promise you an exciting and rewarding journey.

Chapter 1

Personal Encounters

I recall my childhood days with such fondness; such a pleasant mixture of play that was pure fun, often with a sense of meaningfulness. There were social activities, elementary school work and domestic chores. Ironically, there was also an unusual amount of religious activity. A Hindu little girly loved to play church.

Our home was spacious and comfortable, and a popular gathering centre for neighbors and friends who were always welcome.

My father constructed a small two-storey 'doll-house' in the backyard for me. It was a lovely place to play house. But I also used it to play 'church'. I would stand in my "sanctuary" 'preaching' from gospel tracts and talking about God. Imagine me, a small girl, speaking about Him even though I did not yet know who He was, before family members and neighbors many years my senior listening to my homilies.

At special times of the year, such as Easter and Christmas, I kept busy organizing raffles (for fun), concerts, and Christmas parties and plays for the families of the immediate neighborhood. Little did I know that, one day, I would meet this God of the Bible, who seemed to be the centre of my childhood activity, and would preach real messages to real seekers of the Lord Jesus Christ; and would fill my working hours serving Him in a full-scale House of God. What made this early ministry so amazing is that I was a Hindu.

From Hinduism to Christianity

I was born into a Hindu family without a shred of Christian influence. Also, even though my parents were Hindus, I knew very little about Hinduism and its gods. No member of our immediate or extended family ever spoke or boasted about the religion of our birth. The only religious activity in which my parents ever participated was the annual 'prayers' conducted by a Hindu priest. Unfortunately, he took pride in speaking a language none of us understood. None ever taught me to pray or worship until, at the age of twelve, I began attending a Christian Sunday school. I had no personal knowledge of God prior to this time. However, it was there that I began to develop a longing to know Him.

About this time I entered high school; there a series of four spiritual experiences contending for my mind confronted me. First, my best school friend suddenly became involved with a Hindu religious group. She passionately shared her newfound faith with me. Second, one of my teachers took me to a 'Sathya Sai Baba'[1] meeting with the hope of converting me to that cultic faith. Third, at about that same time one of my older sisters, married to a Pentecostal minister, began to share the gospel with me. While I found her testimony very convincing, still, I felt that I needed to choose the God I would serve, and the faith I would embrace. Talk about a real struggle! Fourth, I was introduced to a highly spiritual woman, the grandmother of one of my sisters-in-law, who embraced both Hinduism and Christianity. This woman seemed to have supernatural powers that I found fascinating. I certainly was at cross roads.

Finally, the Lord prevailed; the gospel message won my soul. He used the persistent prayer, and encouragement of my born-again sister (married to the minister). I gladly made Jesus Christ my Lord and Savior. Providentially, I was able to move into the home of my sister shortly after my conversion. At her invitation, I began to attend with a neighborhood congregation, the Diamond Open Bible Church.

Jesus Came Looking for Me

Although the Diamond Open Bible Church was small in membership, its fellowship was especially warm and friendly. The pastor, Reverend Joseph Rostant, was a kind, simple and extremely humble man of God; he embodied the meaning of the phrase, "servant of the Lord".

The brethren in attendance were very friendly; I always felt their deep love for the Lord. My experience in that small assembly was thoroughly enjoyable.

I recall one particular instance, during a Sunday morning worship service, when I had a rather unusual encounter with my Lord. It seemed that Jesus walked into the assembly and stood, as it were, at my side. Tears flowed down my cheeks incessantly. From then on my relationship and love for Jesus grew stronger and stronger. As a result, I began to fall in love with the Lord and devote much time to prayer and fasting. Also, I began to tell others about Him. Whenever I encountered an ill person, a spirit of compassion would overwhelm me. Soon I was laying hands on sick people. I saw the Lord miraculously heal them.

During those early days of conversion from a non-practicing Hindu to a devout Christian, I felt compelled to share the gospel of salvation and healing not just with friends and family but also with many crossing my path. The results of the Lord amazed us all, in spite of the fact that I had no formal training in preaching at that time. Permit me to share one of these experiences.

Once, as I was conducting a "crusade" at our family home, which I did regularly; preaching, testifying and praying for the sick, my unsaved father happened to attend. At the time he was strongly opposed to the Christian faith. Yet, as he entered the room where I was conducting a gospel meeting, tears streamed down his cheeks. It was clear that as he listened to my 'sermon', the Lord was ministering to his spirit with conviction of sin.

As he approached, I felt led of the Lord to lay my hands on him and prayed in the name of Jesus Christ for his healing of rheumatoid arthritis, a disease he had painfully endured for several years, despite monthly visits to the best physicians. He was miraculously healed and shortly thereafter, embraced Christ as His Savior and Lord. My mother's conversion preceded his.

In another of those house meetings, while my family and I were singing and worshipping, there was a wonderful outpouring of the Holy Spirit upon us all. I had just met this Jesus and everything had changed for me: my dreams, my goals, and my aspirations.

Rebuked for Praying for the Sick

After moving back into my parents' home, I joined one of the leading churches in the community, the Penal Open Bible Church. Under the leadership of my new pastor, Reverend Winston Ballosingh, and his wife, Sister Selma, I was challenged and inspired to do exploits for God. Being a woman was neither a problem for them nor a hindrance to them. My pastor, because of his consuming passion for the lost, saw only the 'harvest field' and the untold millions heading to a burning hell. As a result, he never overlooked one single member of his congregation. At every opportunity, he sought to train and develop each one for service in the kingdom of God. I could detect in him no sense of harboring any race, sex or class distinctions. He looked upon every believer under his care as vessels to be filled with the power of God and used for His glory.

As C S Cowles puts it, "all God-called and Spirit-filled potential ministers are 'dead in the water' until someone in a position of authority recognizes their gifts, invites them to participate in increasingly responsible forms of ministry, supports them in times of challenge and encourages them along the way."[2]

My pastor and mentor, Rev Winston Ballosingh, was that someone in a position of authority whom God used to prepare me, and thousands more, for effective ministry on every level.

In my love for souls and my faith in Jesus, I began to heal the sick and deliver the oppressed from Satan's bondage as I began to regularly visit a local hospital in a quest to lead the patients to Christ.

It was at this time that I first encountered opposition to my ministry based on my gender. It occurred one day as I was sharing the gospel with a female patient. Suddenly I was rudely interrupted. I looked up to see a middle-aged man sitting on one of the hospital beds. He was visiting with the patient for whom I was about to pray. He was upset; and the reason was that I, a woman, was sharing the gospel. Interrupting me, he shouted (with a tone of disgust in his voice) that I should desist from what I was doing because, in his view, that was the function of a man.

That was my first encounter with male opposition to females in ministry. It would not be my last. True, I felt intimidated but I vowed not to stop sharing the love of God with a lost generation.

Tongue on Fire: My Calling Experience

A couple of years after my conversion I had a significant supernatural experience. One Sunday, a team of Bible school students, who were assigned to conduct a Bible school recruitment service at our church, visited with us to lead the morning worship service. During the altar call they challenged those who felt a conviction to commence Bible school training. While I did not respond to the call that morning, still, I felt overwhelmed by the presence of the Lord that, following the closure of the service, I went into the church's prayer room to spend some more time in prayer. As I sat there I felt the Lord's presence wrapping me tightly within His strong power. As I lingered in this electric-like moment, I suddenly felt as though a divine hand had placed a live coal of fire on my tongue. I did not fully understand what was happening to me, or the significance of such a strange experience. Later, when I had become familiar with the commission and vision of the prophet Isaiah, I called this an 'Isaiah' experience.[3] Upon leaving the prayer room that morning, I related the incident to my pastor's wife. I can still hear her response, "You'll be a great speaker for God!" Now I can look back and see the hand of the Lord on my life from my conversion onwards.

Warned by the Holy Spirit

About ten years later, I felt pressed in my spirit to visit a small village called Cedros, located at the South Western point of the Island of Trinidad. I did not know why I should go there. But somehow, in my spirit, I knew that this was what the Lord would have me to do. As a result, in obedience, I invited some members of my congregation who worked closely with me in tent evangelism to make the three-hour drive with me.

When we arrived at the small fishing village, I had a strong feeling that I should return later to Cedros with my team, to conduct intercessory prayer meetings and then launch an evangelistic campaign. So I waited until the time was right. That day finally dawned. The group driving with me included seven: Sister Samdaye, who is a longstanding prayer intercessor; a young married couple, (Bobby and Maltee), Sharran, and Sita, the wives of two young pastors, and Nicole, my pastor's daughter. We spent an amazing week together.

While there, God revealed to me the reason He called us to Cedros: to receive a divine commission to move to several other vicinities throughout the Republic of Trinidad & Tobago to break the strongholds of Satan, through prayer-drives and intercessory prayer, and to declare the power of God through evangelistic meetings.

In obedience we conducted such meetings until we had ministered at each place He had shown us. The exercise was completed in approximately nine months.

It was while ministering at Cedros, as my team and I were about to leave our cottage for a crusade, I heard in my spirit that I should prepare myself to be confronted by a man who would show up, solely to interrupt me, by challenging my preaching, since I was a woman.

The Lord led me to the words of Joel, as recorded in Acts 2:16-18:

> "But this is that which was spoken by the prophet Joel; And it shall come to pass in the last days, saith God, I will pour out my Spirit upon all flesh: and your sons and your **daughters shall prophesy**, and your young men shall see visions, and your old men shall dream dreams: and on my servants and on my **handmaidens** I will pour out in those days of my Spirit; and they shall prophesy (emphasis mine)."

Sure enough, at the close of the night's revival, a man came up to me insisting that women ought not to preach. I gently asked him to be seated, opened my Bible to Acts 2:16–18 (KJV) and shared the Scriptures with him.

My hope was that these verses would help him to understand that the call to preach, rendered *prophesy* above, was not restricted to gender.

Apparently, he did. The meetings continued uninterrupted. I never saw the man return.

You Need a Covering

In the year 1993, the Lord directed me to conduct a national prayer mobile throughout Trinidad & Tobago. The prayer mobile was scheduled for May 5th 1993 beginning at the mid-night hour. As I meditated on the assignment, the Lord directed me to seek the help of a certain pastor, whom I knew personally, to assist me in building a national coalition of pastors who would coordinate their congregations to participate. Meeting at his church office, I shared the vision that the Lord had given to me.

I no sooner completed my presentation that he quickly dismissed the possibility that the Lord might ever have prompted my vision since I was an unmarried woman and, therefore, lacked a covering (i.e. male authority to watch over me). He further said that he could not help me in the circumstances. He then offered a short prayer and escorted me to the door.

I was sad and disappointed but remained determined to obey the Lord's bidding. Later, as I reflected on his reaction, I became convinced that he had reacted because he did not want to risk his reputation by working with a woman. I had encountered my second major voice of opposition to my ministry because of me being a woman.

My next option was to approach my own pastor and his wife for their help and support. Reverend Selma Ballosingh, who was widely respected as a leading prayer warrior, did not hesitate to assist me.

From that point onward, everything proceeded smoothly; hundreds of believers joyfully and willingly participated in the national prayer mobile. This army of people would drive through their towns and villages engaging in spiritual warfare. Strongholds of the enemy came crashing down. For this I credit people acting in obedience to God's vision (not a woman's, per se).

"Called but Not Chosen": Recent Confrontation over Gender Issue

A couple of months ago I sat at a table for lunch at a nearby Mall's Food Court. The table seated four, and my spare seats were the only ones available. Noticing two decent-looking gentlemen standing nearby, carrying food trays and looking for seats, I invited them to sit.

Upon being seated, one of the men remarked that it must be the Lord who reserved that space for them and then proceeded to give thanks to God for the meal. Recognizing the men to be Christians, I quickly struck up a conversation with them.

All proceeded well until they learned that I was a pastor. Suddenly the smiles faded. Then one of them began to insist that a woman should be 'silent' in the church. He said that I was 'usurping' the man's 'authority' by publicly declaring the gospel of Jesus Christ and by assuming a leadership role in the church. It was at that point that I took the time to explain to him how I evolved as a minister of the gospel.

I then shared with him how I had come to know the Lord as my Savior in my late teens; how I began a life of prayer and meditation in the Holy Scriptures, attended every service; involved myself in every area of ministry in which I was asked to serve; and began to obey the Word in every way.

I also shared how, after reading Matthew 28:19 ("go and make disciples of all nations,") I had begun to share Christ with others and pray for the sick. I reported the fact of the Lord's miraculous healings. I shared of my calling to Bible school training, and His provision of funds to pay the cost of tuition.

I related how, in my second year at Bible school, when my pastor had encouraged me to preach at the local church and in the surrounding districts, I did not hesitate to engage in teaching, preaching, evangelizing and assisting in the pastorate.

I confessed my great joy at seeing people saved, healed, and strengthened in the faith through my humble service. I invited them to poll my leaders who would testify as to my anointing and giftedness for the work that I had been ordained to carry out. I related how the work had grown in the Lord.

Finally, I confessed that what excited me even more than the growth was the fact that there was an eternal place of punishment (hell) for those who do not know Jesus Christ as their Lord and Savior and a beautiful everlasting place of rest (heaven) for 'the saved' (converts of Christ). I then urged them to appreciate the fact that God needed someone to spread the news—to which I had dedicated my life.

I testified that I enjoyed an international reputation as a pastor, teacher, administrator, leader, and evangelist without exerting any personal effort to build it in the flesh; it was the result of God choosing me to do His work, not personal goals or planning. The men sat silent.

I next asked them, "So tell me, which man's 'authority' am I 'usurping' since I am single (unmarried), and I also have the authorization and blessing of my pastor, who is a man?"

One of them remarked, "Many are called but few are chosen".

It was clear that although I had made my point, their resistance would not change. So standing to leave, I quipped, "When we get on the other side we'll see who was chosen," and quietly took my leave.

The series of events described in this chapter span a period of twenty-five years. The positive experiences were so 'heavenly' and have been beyond comprehension. I can only thank God for my salvation, my unique relationship with Jesus, and my 'Isaiah' experience, the sick He has healed, the lives changed, and especially all of the opposing voices to the legitimacy of my ministry.

With each confrontation, I have gained new insights to affirm the authenticity of my calling. Therefore, I thank God for those experiences as well.

Personally, I have no qualms fulfilling the call of God on my life, even though I have been a target of opposition on several occasions. I am confident of my capability to do the work to which I am called. I also believe that the one who has called me does not take issue with my gender, suitability or competence.

However, for the benefit of other women facing similar challenges, I have opted to make my contribution by writing this book. It is my special pleasure to offer my own experiences as a personal testimony to those of you who, as women called of God to vocational ministry, and more specifically to pastoral ministry, must contend with the voices of opposition.

I pray that the things the Lord has taught me will strengthen your heart and your resolve to accept the truth that women belong in leadership.

ENDNOTES

1 Sathya Sai Baba is believed to be an Avatar or incarnation of God by devotees in India and around the world.
2 C. S. Cowles, *A Woman's Place?: Leadership in the Church* (Beacon Hill Press, 1993), 191-192.
3 Isa 6:1-13.

Chapter 2

Confirmation of My Calling and Giftedness

In a sense, I have always felt somewhat uncomfortable about speaking about a calling. For one thing, few have experienced a calling to ministry. The experience easily falls into subjective issues. In addition, since it is part of a religious experience, people are reluctant to discuss it. Yet, I am compelled to discuss it here, since it figures so importantly into the validation of my own ministry.

False Forms of Calling

First, permit me to share some aspects that I have observed over the past twenty years of ministry that I shall call "false forms of calling."

If people possess a strong talent for public speaking, they will find this profession attractive. After all, they have a captive audience of people who feel it their duty to listen and attempt to understand the message each week. Therefore, if people have such skills, along, say, strong abilities at marketing, they can make a living in either the church, or media ministry.

The profession has another feature that makes it attractive to many people who feel a strong need for the approval of others. The ministry delivers an automatic stamp of goodness to those within the profession.

Another advantage is the financial perks. The job can be handled, slovenly, with only a minimum amount of work executing the essential tasks of "doing church". But if you are concerned about souls and take up the care and nurture of everyone within your congregation the workload stretches to almost two full time units per week (40 hours per week).

In addition, there are opportunities to manipulate people for gifts. Some people, usually out of guilt, or often out of kindness, feel compelled to share objects or cash; and it is tempting to exploit each opportunity, as the falsely called do.

Another financial perk relates to using the church to subsidize expenses that other people have to shoulder. It is easy to use the church finances to cover personal expenses whether they are necessary for ministry or not.

Overall, it can be a financially rewarding job; and the genuinely called must remain vigilant not to be served but to press toward serving.

Often, when uncaring congregations have hurt ministers, they will attempt to isolate themselves from any future pain and take up ministries supported by marketing ventures and which do not require them to submit to the accountability of a church board. These are signs that a genuine calling is beginning to deteriorate.

Difficult to Biblically Verify

Another problem with discussing one's calling is that the Biblical data does not always easily apply to pastoral vocational ministry. When I think of Moses' calling vs. my own, I cannot make a direct connection; his was dramatic, so far reaching in scope. While mine began with a series of small ministry assignments that led to a full calling to a congregation, I never found myself confronted by a burning bush. Yet, when I read of a 'still small voice' speaking to Biblical characters I can identify with this since it typifies the way in which the Holy Spirit spoke to me in successive moments along the way of gaining a full understanding of my calling.

Dr. Bobby Clinton, of Fuller Theological Seminary, describes the typical evolution from a person of faith to a leader of the faithful. He says that it usually moves through a series of stages.

The first stage is where someone in leadership detects that you have the potential for spiritual leadership. They then assign you a series of small tasks. I later learned that the goal of such tasks for me was not just to see if I could accomplish the job, but to determine my tenacity, and faithfulness, and to see if I would do what I promised.

The next stage is where one is given by the spiritual leadership a definite assignment. For me, each of these was at the invitation of my Pastor. Even the ones that the Lord spoke and guided me to attempt were the result of me first going to my pastor to get his approval and blessing; and yes, his counsel and instruction.

The next large step, according to Dr. Clinton, is to be handed a ministry assignment. For me this was a series of long-term responsibilities, including the year long evangelistic campaigns, the long term prayer campaigns, etc.

How I thank God for leading me to such a wonderful, mature pastor, who although he may have never studied Emerging Leadership Development, by J. Robert Clinton, still demonstrated, by the leading of the Spirit that he knew how to develop new believers into called ministry.

At no time did I attempt to abrogate my submission to God by listening to and yielding to the counsel of my pastor. I considered his blessing to be a legitimate covering. I still consider myself, through my ordination, to be serving under his blessing and covering.

Of course I recognize and remain circumspect about the dangers of my calling deteriorating into any of the characteristics I have spoken about as false callings. In no way could anyone have progressed more consistently and typically than my path to full calling. I have read and spoken with many men on this subject and I find my experience typical of almost all men whose lives demonstrate, through their fruit and integrity that they have been genuinely called to ministry.

All of this discussion about "false forms of calling" raises the question, what, exactly, is a call to ministry?

What Is the Call to Ministry?

Joel Nederhood in his intriguing discussion of this in the book, *The Preacher and Preaching,* defines it as a calling to the ministry of the Word and the administering of the Christian ordinances, baptism and communion; a call to a primary church office with the full responsibilities as an overseer and the burden of doing it all in complete obedience to the Lord. It is to be so intimately connected with the Bible that lives in bondage to proclaiming and obeying its precepts. As a result one's life becomes an expression of obedience to the Scripture, and to the Jesus it is all about.

In this regard I think of a verse that stresses this: "So then, men ought to regard us as servants of Christ and people entrusted with the secret things of God" (1 Cor. 4:1, 2).

For me, a full awareness of my calling came as a result of a series of stages. As I share them, perhaps you may sense you are somewhere along the compendium of these stages.

As you observe them you may conclude that they really describe a mature believer, not necessarily a called pastor/leader. At the conclusion of the description of the stages that led to my complete awareness of my calling, I will share one final detail that distinguishes the called from the mature but uncalled.

Stage One: My Conversion

I have already shared much detail about it in chapter one. For me the transformation that the Spirit produced within me was electric. I knew immediately that my life had been changed; that I was His child; and I began to express my love for Him and desire to please him like a new born infant begins to nurse.

Therefore, it was easy for me to speak about it. In the process I was building my "story" into a presentation that could be useful to introduce the Gospel of salvation to lost people. But unless I had been genuinely and radically transformed by the Gospel, no calling would have possibly come to pass.

Stage Two: Consistent Walk

It was a stage I waltzed through with ease because my heart was so filled with love for the Lord. Later, I was to realize that without a consistent walk, any potential for vocational ministry will never see the light of day, since it has been choked and starved to death by a walk that does not feed on the Word.

Stage Three: Passion for the Word

All of the truly called have at least one Word-related gift. This makes sense since the pastoral calling is linked so completely to the ministry of the Word. But where does it begin? It starts with a young emerging leader eager to know the Lord and walk faithfully before Him by turning to the Word. Suddenly you find things that amaze you. You then share them; and the watching leadership, such as my pastor, suddenly takes notice of a person with a strong passion for the Word. This is a strong indicator that this person is a candidate for a calling.

Stage Four: Learning Faithfulness

This is the most essential area to master; to learn to be faithful in little tasks. This is the only legitimate basis for anyone being given larger, more important ministry assignments.

I have already described for you the many ways in which my pastor developed my sense of faithfulness through a series of small tasks and assignments.

Stage Five: Examination of Spiritual Gifts

It is impossible to fulfill a calling to pastoral ministry without one or more of the ministry gifts listed in the Bible in the "Word cluster": teaching, evangelism, knowledge, prophetic gift, to name a few. Early on the pastor recognized my preaching ability and prophesied that I would become a very effective communicator of the Gospel. I feel confident that he would say that his prophetic words have been fulfilled.

Stage Six: Calling Meets Service

Actually this is the one area that distinguishes the called from the otherwise mature Christian.

Upon reflection, I have reduced a large list to the following attitudes that I feel are unique to the person who is called:

1. Obedience to Jesus that leads me to hurt when they hurt and love serving them, and being comfortable with an attitude of self-sacrifice; think of it as a willingness to become Christ' earthly representative. I believe this was what Paul meant when he counseled the Elders at the Ephesian church:

> "Guard yourselves and the flock of which the Holy Spirit has made you overseers. Be shepherds of the church of God, which He bought with His own blood" (Acts 20:28).

I think those called to ministry have a consciousness of the magnitude of the task that enables them to understand the level of obedience required to fulfill this calling.

2. Self-Discipline: The calling of God requires an enormous amount of self-discipline in every area of one's life including one's devotional time, habits, and even exercise.

3. Self-sacrifice: This includes a willingness to endure hardship in terms of finances, peer pressure, and even physical comfort.

4. Self-giving: The best way to demonstrate that one lives by faith is by sharing with the needy.

5. Self-control: This is very important because the ministry can bring one into situations where propriety is most important. This is often the one area that can ruin one's reputation and wreck a calling on an individual.

Over the years, my calling has expressed itself in different ways. What I, early on, experienced as an internal calling has been repeatedly verified, externally, not just by my Pastor, but also by those who minister with me and by the countless fruit that has resulted from my twenty plus years of living out my calling.

Now you have a broad view of the key points in my development as one called to ministry. You also have a good idea of the nature of the opposition I have continually faced from people seeking to restrict my calling to vocational ministry.

With this background, I will now deal with the terms and concepts which are used in an attempt to limit women's ministerial leadership. To this extent I will focus on two terms, 'calling' and 'gifting,' and then clarify three concepts: 'silencing of women,' 'spiritual covering,' and 'usurping authority.' I will use these terms to establish the arguments that not only are the two terms not limited to gender, but that it is largely tradition, culture, and the misinterpretation of Scripture that are responsible for fueling the antagonism towards women in higher church leadership. We shall probe this strategic term from three vantages: Webster's Dictionary, counsel of a theologian, and a careful exegesis of the terms 'calling' and 'giftedness.'

Calling

When one sees the body of ministry to the church in the areas of preaching, teaching, evangelizing and leading over the past two decades that I have consistently rendered not just to my congregation, but to the body of Christ nationally, as well as internationally, could any rational person not conclude that such fruit could only be the result of God having selected me for preaching and teaching responsibilities as a leader/pastor of a congregation?

Not having been born into a pastor's home, or being a bishop's niece, I started at ground zero. At every step, God prompted me, often through the leading of my pastors to special ministry tasks. At every juncture I served faithfully, and received their approval and appreciation. There was not one area of ministry that I did not approach from the bottom, learn it thoroughly, and lead others to do, including personal evangelism, individual witnessing and mass evangelism. I have led teams, conducted many Bible classes, and filled many pulpits, preaching and teaching the Word of God. I have learnt every aspect of organizational leadership including strategic planning.

Is it even conceivable that one could sustain such a level of ministry, against such opposition, and with such skill, and focus, and discipline for twenty years without a special 'calling'? The answer lies, in part, in understanding the meaning of the word 'calling'.

Webster defines "calling" as (1), "a strong inner impulse toward a particular course of action especially when accompanied by conviction of divine influence" and (2), "the vocation or profession in which one customarily engages."[4] My life and work to date is characterized by nothing less.

Next, I will seek the insights of Dr. Ann L. Bowman, assistant professor of Biblical studies at International School of Theology. She has written of "abundant examples of individuals called into God's service." Not just the mighty giants, Abraham, Moses, The Apostles, and Paul, but also individuals such as Deborah, Stephen, Philip, and Barnabas, as well as such women as Phoebe (Rom. 16:1-2), Priscilla (Acts 18:26), Tabitha (Acts 9:36-42), and Lydia (Acts 16:13-15).

All of these people fulfilled God's call on their lives." [5]

Hebrew Word for "Calling" (*Miqra*)

The word we associate with "calling of God", comes from the word, דקְרָא *qara' I* (kha-RAH-ah) which means "to call, invoke, summon, proclaim, appeal to. The noun is דמִקְרָא , *miqra'*) (MI-crah) which means, one who is summoned, delegated, called to proclaim.

The meaning of this root word is to draw attention to oneself by using your voice to make contact with someone else. Other uses of the word include to extend an invitation, or to summon to a special purpose, as to war, or to court.

From these the theologically important usage emerged with God as subject; the meaning is "to call one into the service of the Lord". The idea is that when the Lord calls people, He is declaring His sovereignty over them, His taking possession of them for a special use in a special service.

It also means that He takes full responsibility for their actions, and to be behind their actions. It signifies that as a result of this calling, a close relationship now exists between the called person, and the Lord who executed the calling.

Greek Word for "Calling"

We begin with a brief analysis of the word καλεο (kah-LEH-oh). The word means to speak to another person either directly or through an intermediary, in order to bring the person nearer, either physically or to establish a personal relationship. From this word we get our word for "calling".

In regard to the word for calling, the Greek word ***παρακλκητοσ*** fits the bill. It means to invite a person in as a welcome guest. This invitation conveyed special honor. As a result, the word evolved into the concept of "to be chosen." With this, the word conveys the meaning of an official summons by a recognized authority (e.g., military, or governmental) and so means "calling" altogether.

When used in reference to a divine calling, the noun takes on the idea of claiming and commissioning. This use of the word by the New Testament writers introduced a brand new use of the word. This is because in secular Greek society, the term for professional services was ***εργον***, i.e., ***ergon***.

The New Testament writers attached the idea of a vocational calling. It identifies those who devote themselves to specialized callings, such as the Gospel ministry, either as apostles, prophets, evangelists, and pastors and teachers.

It does denote a position higher in rank; therefore, it was always associated with being a command (summons) not a self-directed invitation.

Also, the idea inherent in its meaning is that the invitation must not be ignored or refused.

Further, this call often leads to suffering for God's sake. It also must be accompanied by devotion and dedication in service. Before a man can answer, he must realize that the call he has heard comes from God. Young Samuel typifies the calling of God, and the need to verify that the calling is actually from God (I Sam. 3:4-10).

This act of calling demands a decision from the one being addressed. Also, this calling is the means by which God transforms unqualified people into instruments of His will.

In the New Testament, the word occurs nearly 150 times. It is used in regard to the calling of Paul, the Apostle. The Gospel writer that uses the word the most is Luke; and the reason is that he came from a Greek background and possessed a sufficiently sophisticated understanding of the term to use it in this specialized context.

Paul understood calling as the process by which God calls those, whom He has already elected and appointed, out of their bondage to this world, into His service. It brings the one called into fellowship with Christ (1 Cor. 1:9).

He also uses the word in relation to his own personal commission as an apostle. His point was to stress that he owed his office as apostle to a special call by God. Those called by him are to bear witness to the One who had called them out of darkness (1 Pet. 2:9) by following the example of Christ even in suffering (2:21), so that they may inherit a blessing (3:9; cf. 2 Pet. 1:3 f.).

Giftedness

One of the more important indicators of my call to leading/pastoral ministry has been from the response of respected leaders about me who acknowledge the persistent strong evidence that I possessed the clusters of spiritual gifts uniquely associated with pastoral ministry. These include the Word cluster (teaching, knowledge, and prophecy); Counseling cluster (discernment, helps, and mercy), and the leading cluster (leading, presiding, and eldership).

I have studied much about spiritual gifts because I see one of my main tasks in ministry as the call to discern potential and develop emerging leaders. The only legitimate basis for someone being appointed to a spiritual ministry task or responsibility is that you detect, in them, some evidence of an appropriate spiritual gift. I have even taken formal training in this subject at a graduate level. I mentioned all of this to demonstrate my understanding of what spiritual gifts are, and the roles they play in revealing a person for a true ministry, such as leader/pastor.

I once read that spiritual gifts can initially be detected, even among unsaved people, by the skills they use to fulfill the interests to which they are drawn. I now see that as why, although a young girl, I used my house to 'plant' a 'church', and pursue a full schedule of events I now fulfill professionally for the congregation I serve.

More importantly, from the outset of my Pastor's repeated invitations to serve in one capacity or another, he, and the maturely spiritual people about him would smile, knowingly, "yes, Kay certainly has the right mix of spiritual gifts, doesn't she?" I know this to be true because they would usually make similar comments to me. Also, I recognized, early on, that whenever I was placed by God and the Pastor (under whose covering I have always, spiritually, served), those who were selected to serve with me, and become accountable to me for planning and execution, recognized this. I know this to be true, for they all would gladly and willingly respond to my leadership. This is a very important indicator of one possessing the spiritual gifts of leading. When I would study in the Word, incredible insights would come to mind. I often had to stop and just worship the Lord for these insights. Also, when I would present them, the spiritual response showed me that the fit was accompanied by significant anointing.

Therefore, from the outset I have enjoyed four independent sources confirming my leader/pastor giftedness:

i) from my pastoral leadership;
ii) from those I served in the capacity of being their leader (i.e., servant leader);
iii) the copious amount of fruit that the exercise of my gifts generated; and,
iv) the way in which my gift revealed aspects of itself during my childhood.

I am so grateful for this because in addition to the very evident calling to my ministry, I treasure the way in which I am able to perform all aspects of the leader/pastoral ministry with ease, joy, and effectiveness with which I am privileged to function. I truly live a blessed life because I know where I belong, and I am gifted for it—surely a clear indication of the leading of the Lord in my life. (And look where He led me—to pastoral leadership).

There are many definitions of a spiritual gift, but I am fond of the one offered by theologian and preacher, Lewis Sperry Chafer. He defines a spiritual gift, in the Biblical sense of it, as a direct undertaking or manifestation of the Spirit working through the believer by the energy and power of the Holy Spirit to accomplish a spiritual goal. Notice what this does NOT mean: it is not a believer accomplishing something and calling on God for help in the task. Rather it is the Holy Spirit doing something through the believer to accomplish His will.[6]

I have also been blessed with the way in which other outstanding Christian leaders identify the kinds of gifts. Loren Cunningham, founder of *Youth With A Mission*, and David Joel Hamilton in their book *Why Not Women,* identifies three kinds of gifts: natural gifts, Holy Spirit-imparted gifts, and ministry gifts."[7]

Cunningham & Hamilton describe a natural gift as more akin to a talent one might be born with. I think of Ezekiel who was a gifted singer. They point to Isaiah as a gifted speaker/writer: "*Before I was born* the LORD called me. . . . He made my mouth like a sharpened sword." One might include in this group Jeremiah who was also called from the womb to be a prophet to the nations.[8] So how does the emerging spiritual leader move from the use of his talent to the exercise of spiritual gifts?

I like the way Cunningham & Hamilton explain this transition. They write, "As we stay submitted to God and His call, He allows us to go beyond our natural gifts. He releases Spirit-imparted gifts for specific occasions, for specific individuals, and for specific needs."[9]

They then listed the gifts found in 1 Corinthians 12:8-10 which they describe as Spirit-imparted gifts:

- the word of wisdom through the Spirit
- the word of knowledge
- the gift of faith
- gifts of healing

- the ability to work miracles
- prophecy
- the ability to distinguish spirits
- various kinds of tongues
- the ability to interpret an unknown tongue

They say, "The other category of New Testament gifts –the ministry gifts –has to do with **function** (emphasis mine) in the body of Christ,"[10] and that it is God who has "put these gifts in the body according to His will."[11] According to them, the gifts of ministry or function are:

- the apostle
- the prophet
- the evangelist
- the pastor
- the teacher
- the one who serves
- the exhorter
- the giver
- the leader
- the one who shows mercy
- the helper
- the administrator
- the preacher
- other giftings[12]

The Bible tells us that our gifts come from God (Eph 4:8). It also says that "God's gifts and his call are irrevocable" (Rom 11:29).[13] The Apostle Paul identifies the most strategically important gifts for leadership ministry as apostolic, prophetic, evangelistic, and pastoral gifts (Eph 4:8): ". . . his gifts were that some should be apostles, some prophets, some evangelists, some pastors and teachers" (Eph. 4:11).[14]

On the surface, according to the English version of the Bible, it appears that these gifts are intended for a specific gender "...given by God to men**".** Nevertheless, one must question, do we get our Scriptural authority from a primary or a secondary source? Is it possible to determine, honestly, if these most important leadership gifts are only meant for men, or does the text provide a legitimate argument that they were also intended for women?

The answer is yes, and I shall fully develop it by analyzing, in depth, the above phrase in the language in which the apostle Paul wrote it. In fact, in chapter four, I shall deal with every verse that the Detractors use to argue me out of vocational ministry.

In that chapter, I will share the observations of Loren Cunningham and David Joel Hamilton, in their book, *"Why Not Women?"* We shall resolve any and all doubt about whether this passage excludes any woman, including me, with demonstrated giftedness, and time tested effective evidence from being called, gifted, and used to preach, teach, lead, administrate, evangelize and pastor, and to do everything that God has called and gifted us to do.

However, before I proceed to this powerful data, I feel it most important to provide you with the philosophical basis for the opposition. Their view is built on a concept, conceived by Socrates, that dominated the Western World, and then was "Christianized" by such giants of church history as Thomas Aquinas, John Calvin, and then, through their influence, has been fed into the living water systems from which every modern Bible school serves to its students.

Brace yourself, the argument is about to turn, well, uh, crazy".

ENDNOTES

4 A. Merriam-Webster, Webster's New Collegiate Dictionary (G. & C. MERRIAM COMPANY, Springfield, Massachusetts, U.S.A., 1980).

5 James R. Beck & Craig L. Blomberg, *Two Views On Women In Ministry,* 244 (Grand Rapids, Michigan: Zondervan Publishing House, 2001).

6 Lewis Sperry Chafer, *He That Is Spiritual* (Grand Rapids: Zondervan, 1967), 54. Quoted in Craig & Blomberg, 263.

7 Loren Cunningham & David Joel Hamilton with Janice Rogers, *Why Not Women? A Fresh Look At Scripture On Women In Missions, Ministry, and Leadership (*Seattle, WA: YWAM Publishing, 2000) 46.

8 Jer. 1:5.

9 Cunningham & Hamilton, 49.

10 Ibid. , 50.

11 Ibid.

12 Scriptural references to the gifts listed above can be found in Ro. 10:14; 12:6-8; 1 Co. 12:10, 27-31; Eph. 4:11; 1 Pet. 4:9-11 (NIV).

13 Nestle- Aland, *Greek - English New Testament,* Editio XXV11.

14 Ibid.

PART TWO:
Winning the War of the Word

Cultural Roots and Biblical Errors of Detractor Arguments

An Overview of each Chapter's Content

Introduction

Every detractor confronting me over the past two decades has used one of four Biblical passages to support their argument that, on principle, the Scripture prohibits women from positions of pastoral leadership, including me.

A few years ago, the Lord led me to graduate school. There I discovered many helpful insights regarding ministry. Among the more important subjects, I consider the courses on Expositional Hermeneutics, Hebrew and Greek Exegesis to be very helpful.

After learning the rules for correct Biblical interpretation, I experienced a new apprehension. I feared that, after a correct analysis of the four primary passages, I might learn that those four Scriptural passages continually thrown at me did disqualify women from ministry leadership.

To resolve this worry, I took two steps. First, I made a gut-wrenching decision. I yielded the problem to the Lord, telling Him that if, after careful research, I discovered that my 'Detractors' interpretations were true, after all, then I would resign from my pastoral position. That spiritual experience ushered in a settled peace. Second, I then threw myself into an in-depth research of each of the passages related to women's issues. I later wrote my doctoral dissertation on the research that grew out of that concentrated investigation. Much of this information is the basis for the chapters of Part Two. Permit me to sketch the direction of this major section that spans four chapters, and provide you a brief idea of the content of each chapter.

Chapter 3: Overview of the Information Presented in Part Two

In this brief chapter we shall introduce the reader to the process by which legitimate Biblical analysis is conducted using the laws of Hermeneutics. Then, we will provide a brief synopsis of the key passages that are used to debate the issue of women in leadership.

Chapter 4: Cultural and Historical Roots of Detractor's Argument

There are two lenses through which one can view the writing of the apostles. The first is that which begins with Socrates and moves historically through the Rabbinical writings, then to the Pharisees, and then on to Aquinas and Calvin to the modern era. At first this lens seems to produce the strongest rationale for excluding women from ministry leadership. However, once you trace its roots back to Socrates you discover just how corrupt and antagonistic to the Scriptures were its roots.

The other lens is to view the Scripture through the lens of expositional exegesis. We shall, in this chapter, trace the historical path of that first lens, and then, in subsequent chapters, view the true Biblical basis for resolving this issue using the Bible itself.

Chapter 5: Corinthian Passages (1 Cor. 11 and 14)

In this chapter we introduce the reader to the religious and cultural background in which the Corinthian church functioned—the sexual cult of Astarte. Once you grasp this background you will understand how Paul in chapter eleven addresses the issue of headship, and in chapter 14, the issue of women keeping silent, and living under the covering of a headship.

Chapter 6: Ephesian Related Passages (1 Tim. 2 and Eph. 4)

In this chapter we will introduce the reader to the unique cultural matrix in which the Church at Ephesus existed. This understanding will provide the reader with a sense of why Paul was speaking to the congregation regarding women. Small wonder since the religious life of the city was dominated by a female led religion. From this perspective you will be able to appreciate Paul's counsel regarding women usurping authority (1 Tim.2) and the calling of women to vocational ministry (Eph. 4) both written to this congregation pastored by Timothy.

Chapter 7: Final Look at Critical Issues

Since we have analyzed, in detail, each of the four controversial passages that related to the argument of women in leadership, we need to step back and view the issues in a non-exegetical context. In this chapter, we summarize our thoughts on "head-covering", "women keep silent", "women usurping authority", and "women called to leadership ministry". Of course we will pull together, in capsule form, all of the important points our detailed analyses in chapters 5 and 6 uncovered. However, we want to share some important information not covered in an exegetical analysis.

With this overview in mind, let us proceed to visit each of these pieces of the puzzle that will resolve this argument better than I have ever been able to do in the emotion of being confronted with them.

Now that we have this map to mark our logical path, let us begin our journey to unravel the meaning of the key Biblical passages that make up the theological war of the Word over women in leadership.

Chapter 3

Understanding the Process of Our Analysis

Introduction

Throughout my ministry I have faced the arguments of men and women who felt I was usurping the office of pastor/leader. I have related some of the incidents in my initial testimonial. Recall the gentleman who confronted me during the Cedros Crusade who sought to silence my preaching of the gospel on the grounds of my gender.

By his demeanor, I sensed that he was sincere in arguing against me preaching. His position was based on his belief that Scripture restricts the public ministry of women; in other words, "women should remain silent in the churches".[15] He believed that I was violating the Word of God; therefore, he felt compelled to persuade me to stop preaching at the crusade. In my naiveté I lacked the Biblical knowledge to argue with him; so I could only read a Biblical passage I knew which support my cause, Acts 2:17-18, and then leave him to meditate on the meaning of its message.

Years later, while reading Linda Bellevue, I understood something as to why this courteous man cared to confront me in the first place? In *Two Views on Women in Ministry*, she remarks,

> "One of the continuing hotbeds of debate in evangelical circles today is the nature and scope of leadership roles open to women in the church. Can she preach God's word, marry, bury and baptize? Can she serve as the senior or solo pastor?"[16]

Other writers, Stanley J. Grenz & Denise Muir Kjesbo, in *Women in the Church: A Biblical Theology of Women in Ministry,* relate how this debate captured the 1986 meeting of the Evangelical Theological Society. The issue discussed was, "Male and Female in Biblical and Theological Perspective". As a result two major competing coalitions formed. One group took the name of "Christians for Biblical Equality." The competing group adopted the name, "Council on Biblical Manhood and Womanhood."[17]

Christians for Biblical Equality advocated that God called and gifted persons into all aspects of public ministry without regard for their gender. Theirs became known as the egalitarian position.

In the words of James R. Beck and Craig L. Blomberg, General Editors of *Two Views on Women in Ministry,* Egalitarians stress the "*equality* of men and women, not merely for salvation or in essential personhood, but in opportunities to hold every office and play every role that exists in church life."[18]

In opposition, the Council on Biblical Manhood and Womanhood believed that "the Bible places restrictions on the public ministry of women."[19] Their position became known as the *traditionalist position.* (It has since been renamed as the "complementarian" view).[20] The Traditionalists or *hierarchialists* "favor certain timeless restrictions on women's roles in the church."[21]

Belleville says, "Many traditionalists still claim that theirs is the 'Christ-honoring, Bible-believing perspective' and that the egalitarian perspective is the "liberal, culturally acceptable view." [22] But what does the passage itself say?

Her question will serve as the guiding light of this chapter. We shall now confront the most prominent Biblical verses used to support those opposed to women in leadership roles of ministry. It follows, logically, upon the heels of our discussion of the last chapter where I traced the cultural roots of the opposition.

As you can see, the ideas that produced the opposing arguments have sordid philosophical headwaters, don't they? Again, this is not to say that my Detractors would embrace all of the evil implications that gave life to their viewpoints. In fact, I feel these people are sincere, and embrace their positions sincerely, and out of ignorance of the true roots of their cause.

I concluded that last chapter on the cultural roots of my Detractors' arguments eager to plunge into this one so that I can tackle the verses which are used by this bankrupt position to support its arguments.

I must say I welcome this debate. I know these verses well, since they have been hurled at me from every angle over the past two decades of ministry. That is understandable since all agree that these passages deal with the issue of women in ministry leadership. This will provide boundaries to resolve this argument by properly interpreting the meaning of these passages.

However, resolution will only be possible as a result of three things. First, the results must be derived by the application of sound hermeneutical laws and following their exegetical process. This means I cannot yield to the temptation to engage in eisegesus (building a textual interpretation by making the words fit my preconceived viewpoint). Interestingly, Hermeneutics is the only genuinely scientific course taught in seminary. It earns this distinction since its principles are derived by deductive logic and replicable in the laboratory, classroom, or Pastor's Study.

Second, I must not bring to the process any preconceived notions of what the interpretation should be. This is not easy because I have wrestled with this issue and these passages so much it is hard to lay aside what I already believe. Yet, by limiting myself to the scientific process of sound expositional exegesis I can achieve this goal.

This fear is not new. When I first sat in exegesis classes in my Masters program, I would ask myself, "What if these principles, when applied to the appropriate Biblical passages proved that I did NOT belong in pastoral ministry? To deal with this fear I would go before the Lord and confess my willingness to abide the accurate interpretation. Even now, on the threshold of this investigation, I am finding it difficult to exhale. Actually, surrendering my destiny to the Word of God was nothing new because my whole ministry has been built upon the Word of God. So it made perfect sense that in this matter I could not allow anything to stand in the way to living by faith in obedience to the Scriptures.

Third, I must first submit myself to the Lord to accept what the hermeneutical laws determine to be the correct interpretation of each passage. To that end, I must resolve that if I should find their argument to be legitimately supported by Scripture, I will resign from vocational pastoral ministry. I confess that should that occur, I would be lost, since fulfilling my calling in vocational ministry has been my life since I was a teenager. To appreciate my situation, think of me as a surgeon attempting to save his own child's life.

Today I rejoice that the Body of Christ possesses such valuable tools so it can establish with scientific accuracy the true interpretation of each Biblical passage, including those relevant to the female ministry issue. They make it impossible for a detractor to argue, "Well you can make the Bible say anything", as a way of dismissing the validity of an opposing argument. Truth is, each Bible passage does have one meaning which is the one the author intended to convey. For this, we have Hermeneutics.

Expositional Hermeneutical Process

Before I proceed to analyze each Biblical passage, I feel that you, dear reader, need to understand the essence of Biblical interpretation. As I mentioned above, in my graduate training I completed several courses in this field, including Biblical Hermeneutics, Exegetical principles, and even Hebrew and Koine Greek. What I learned so strengthened my ability to properly interpret a passage of Scripture that I can say it transformed my pulpit ministry.

So what are the rules of sound Biblical exegesis? Permit me to provide you with a cursory understanding of three key aspects of this process which Biblical scholars, since the apostles, have used to arrive at the true meaning of a Biblical passage.

Understanding the Laws of Biblical Interpretation

Uniqueness of the Bible

It is my conviction that the Bible is God's Word to mankind, fully inspired by God and totally complete in its message. It was written by forty men who came from varying backgrounds and lived in different times and cultures. It was also written over a long period of time, approximately one and a half millennia. It includes history, prophecy, poetry, prose, song, parables, riddles, types and shadows, symbolism, and every imaginable figure of speech found in the English language.

Because of its divine and human authorship, the Bible is authoritative as well as historical. It is authoritative in that it states what God wants. It is historical in that its human influence is tied to specific cultures and times of history. The Bible gives direction and instruction and is the ultimate and final authority on God and man. The unity of the Book is seen in the one grand theme that runs through the sixty-six books of the Bible, the story of man's redemption.

Even though large portions of the Bible are straightforward and easy to understand, there are some passages that present some difficulty. The Apostle Peter, speaking of the Apostle Paul's writings, said, "His letters contain some things that are hard to understand, which ignorant and unstable people distort, as they do the other Scriptures, to their own destruction."[23]

Therefore, while major doctrines relating to God, man, sin, and salvation are generally clear and repetitious, the Bible is not altogether a simple book. Four key factors impact one's ability to correctly interpret the meaning of any Biblical passage: the Language Factor, the Context Factor, the Cultural Factor, and the Historical Factor. Let us examine these contributing factors responsible for the lack of ease in Bible interpretation.

The Language Factor

The Bible was written originally in Hebrew and Greek. As translators worked to rewrite it in today's languages, they no doubt had to grapple with differences in grammar, tenses, moods, sentence construction, and noun and verb systems. For instance, Hebrew (the original language of the Old Testament) was written from right to left. Its sentences were constructed with consonants only, without spaces between words.

Getting the Passage Right

The division of the Bible into chapters and verses and the insertion of punctuation marks came later, as translators tried to facilitate quotation and better understanding of the material. For example, with respect to chapter divisions, some interpreters believe that the great love chapter of the Bible, 1 Corinthians 13, should really begin with the last verse of the preceding chapter. So it matters that one does not include the true unit of meaning (paragraph level) by depending on the chapter divisions in the English translation.

Getting the Punctuation Right

Also, one must consider the matter of punctuation. Take this passage as an example. In the punctuation of Isaiah 59:19b in the King James Version of the Bible this verse reads, ". . . When the enemy shall come in like a flood, the Spirit of the Lord shall lift up a standard against him." Some interpreters suggest that the comma following *flood* is misplaced. In their view, the comma should be placed after *in* causing the verse to look like this: ". . . When the enemy shall come in, like a flood the Spirit of the Lord shall lift up a standard against him." The former quotation likens the entrance of the *enemy* to a flood whereas the latter likens the work of the *Spirit of the Lord* to a flood. Punctuation makes a huge difference

Analysis of the Meaning of Any Passage

Interpreting a Biblical passage requires analyzing it in the language in which it was written; otherwise one is attempting to arrive at a true meaning based on second hand data. This analysis involves three components: the morphological, syntactical, and semantic interpretations.

The morphological interpretation deals with the meaning of the word itself. This includes its root meaning; and the etymological aspects of its development.

The syntactical aspect of interpretation deals with the meaning of the word in the sentence in which it occurs. This is vital so that not only the core meaning can be understood, but also the meaning the word has in the specific sentence in which it occurs.

The final aspect requires the data from the two previous analytical processes to conduct the semantic analysis, drawing conclusions based on the data gleaned to determine the author's intended meaning. However, before the syntactical analysis process is concluded we must understand the contextual factor.

The Context Factor

It is also impossible to properly interpret a Biblical passage without dealing with the contextual factor, as this following example with illustrate.

In the Greek language (the original language of the New Testament), there are some words that may not have a specific meaning unless those words are seen in their contexts. For example, the Greek used the word *aner* for both 'man' and 'husband' and the word *gune* for both 'woman' and 'wife.' For this reason it becomes necessary to refer to the original languages for the specific meaning of words used in the difficult passages of Scripture.

It is not uncommon to find people who search the Scriptures for proof texts to support their traditional and cultural beliefs. Here are two more examples. Firstly, in 1 Corinthians 15 Paul addressed a major problem in the church. The doctrine of the resurrection of the dead was being called into question. Some false teachers were promoting the idea that there was no resurrection for the dead.

In correcting the problem, Paul showed the inconsistency of those false teachers at Corinth who denied the doctrine of the resurrection, but accepted the fallacy of baptism for the dead. Yet there are people who base their support for the belief that one can be baptized for the dead, on 1 Corinthians 15:29 (NKJV), which says, ". . . what will they do who are baptized for the dead, if the dead do not rise at all? Why then are they baptized for the dead?" This is a simple case of ignoring proper principles of interpretation, and taking a verse out of context and using it as a proof text for an erroneous belief. To get a good grasp of Paul's argument in favor of the resurrection, one must look at the entire chapter of 1 Corinthians 15, which would be referred to as the broad context.

Permit me to share a second example that arises in Colossians 2:21(NKJV): "Do not touch, do not taste, do not handle," which is used as a basis for legalism. Let us look at this verse in the context in which it was used.

> Therefore, if you died with Christ from the basic principles of the world, why, as though living in the world, do you subject yourselves to regulations—Do not touch, do not taste, do not handle, which all concern things which perish with the using- according to the commandments and doctrines of men? These things indeed have an appearance of wisdom in self-imposed religion, false humility, and

> neglect of the body, but are of no value against the indulgence of the flesh. (Colossians 2:20- 23, NKJV)

In this Colossian passage Paul is actually decrying legalism not sanctioning it. He was admonishing the church to be free of the doctrine of men and not be entangled with it.

Fortunately, this insight becomes known by dealing with the contextual issues.

Are you now convinced that the right application of hermeneutical rules produces right interpretation? Imagine the mess if such rules did not exist! For instance, the statement "there is no God," is found fifteen times in the Bible. It is not until you look at each one in context that you realize that they are all part of a sentence to the effect of "there is no God but one" in Deuteronomy 32:39 (NIV) or "the fool says in his heart, there is no God" in Psalm 14:1(NIV). Think about it; without dealing with the contextual factor, one might conclude that the Bible is dominated by an atheistic theme.

The story is told about a man who wanted a word from God. As he parted the pages of the Bible his eyes fell on Matthew 27:5 (KJV), "And he cast down the pieces of silver in the temple, and departed, and went and hanged himself." He was not pleased with that verse so he turned again and found, ". . . Go, and do thou likewise" (Luke 10:37, KJV). He thought he had missed God again and decided to try one last time. This time his eyes fell on John13:27 (KJV) ". . . That thou doest, do quickly." What a way to read God's Word, and yet there are some who do the same, pulling verses out of context and making them gospel truth.

Before I leave this discussion of the contextual factor, I need to deal with one aspect of it that is important enough that we have devoted one entire chapter to it: the cultural factor.

The Cultural Factor

As you may be aware, the analysis of a Biblical passage also involves understanding the historical and cultural context in which it was written. This is why we have grouped the four Biblical passages into two groups, each involving a separate cultural context.

However, we shall first trace the cultural roots of the argument that contends that women do not belong in ministry leadership. Where did all of these ideas originate? This we shall shortly discover in the next chapter.

The Historical Factor

To properly understand the Bible – its historical background, time periods, cultures, and geography, we must rely on honest church historians to help bridge the gaps and assist in the recreation of the original setting. More than two thousand years have passed since the last book of the Bible was written. Since that time much change has taken place: language has changed, the meaning of words has changed, culture has changed, and the world has changed. The key therefore in Bible interpretation is to know the difference between truth for all time and truth relative to a particular situation so that we can apply the Word to our own lives.

The Pauline Epistles, which were written to solve existing problems in the local churches, and to address specific issues, are a case in point. It is only as we read the letters that we come to understand what the problems were. But despite all the hermeneutical tools available today, exegetes are still baffled with some difficult verses of Scripture. Yet the Bible is its own best interpreter, for Scripture interprets Scripture. A good example of this is our inability to understand the book of Revelation independent of the book of Daniel. For this reason it is absolutely necessary for us to apply scientific rules or hermeneutical principles when interpreting Scripture.

There are several more hermeneutical[24] principles that should be observed to facilitate proper exegesis. However, that is not our focus; we only need to understand enough on the subject to appreciate the process we shall now explain.

There is one more thing you need to appreciate: what the whole argument is about.

The Issue Central to All Other Issues: Women and the Gift of Prophecy

The issue of women in leadership centers about the gift of prophecy, since it is a gift designed to be exercised before the entire congregation. Therefore, if a woman possesses this spiritual gift, she can only exercise it in public ministry, so she must be called to ministry leadership. This will become clear as we discover what the gift entails, and the Apostle Paul's insistence that women possess and exercise this gift.

Prophesying is the expounding of the mind of God with application to the specific problems of the day. When it is done properly hearts are greatly blessed. But when it is mishandled, it can result in dry profundity and boring theologizing. Paul addresses the misuse of the gift cluster. This term embraces all use of the Word gift in a public setting. So when we highlight it as the prophetic gift, we include using it to teach, evangelize, and to counsel. However, the gifts of teaching and evangelism have universal implications; it is possible to exercise these without being in vocational ministry. In contrast, the gift of prophesying is not universal.

Uniqueness of Prophecy

Prophecy has to do with taking the words of Scripture and communicating them as the very words of God—which, in fact, they are. Its goal also extends beyond imparting information. It seeks to change hearts, minds and wills—to move people to change their ways, to repent from their current life to choose to trust and obey the Person of Christ, and His Word, as the will and direction for their life.

When men say they have been called to preach, this realization occurs after the recognition of the prophetic gift. I know because I experienced this same calling. I say this with confidence because I know the Biblical references where Paul speaks of the right of women to exercise this gift; therefore, they must legitimately possess it.

With these facts as a backdrop, we are ready to deal with the specific verses that will show, in a composite picture, the full extent of this truth. Biblical references that deal with this issue are localized in four primary passages of Scripture. I will now share these, then explain the rules for decoding their meaning, and then speak to another aspect of meaning—the cultural piece of the interpretative puzzle.

Argument from Scripture Used by "Male Only Ministers" Advocates

Every person who has ever confronted me with the goal of dissuading me from continuing my calling in ministry leadership has made reference to one or more of four key verses. Therefore, I will use this opportunity to answer them by providing a clear analysis of each Biblical passage. However, in this chapter, I will mention them briefly and point out the key issues we shall address.

Biblical Passage #1: 1 Cor. 11:2-16
The question one needs to answer is what is the meaning of the term "head" as used in Paul's day?

Biblical Passage #2: 1 Cor. 14:26-40
The critical issues to be resolved include, woman keeping silent—does it mean that women are not to exercise the prophetic gift in leading the full assembly in praying and preaching.

Biblical Passage #3: Ephesians 4:8, 11, 12
The critical issue is, does the word, "men" mean members of the male gender.

Biblical Passage #4: I Timothy 2:8-15
This passage is a goldmine, dealing with several issues.

Interestingly, these four passages can be dealt with as two groups since two of them were written to the Corinthian church and the other two were addressed to the church at Ephesus (since Timothy, to whom 1 Timothy was written, was the pastor of this church). In adapting this approach we also can see these four passages from a cultural (contextual) perspective. All we need to analyze regarding the two First Corinthian passages we will present in Chapter Five; likewise, all that pertains to the Ephesian congregation, in Chapter Six.

Conclusion

As I have presented the Gospel to thousands of people over the years, I have learned that I cannot convince any non-believer who willfully refuses to accept the truth, or any believer who refuses to accept the results of sound interpretation.

I wish those who assert, "So what, I can make the Bible support any argument," would stop to think about this implication: without a true interpretation process, there can be no sound doctrine, therefore, no basis for our faith, or any power to our preaching. The promises we share with the lost, like drowning victims, would not be worth the paper on which they were written.

Therefore, this debate is not a friendly exchange of ideas; I am fighting for the character of God who wrote the Book and declared its promises as "the Words of life".

Regarding this debate, permit me to set up the next discussion by making an observation and asking a question. Observation: currently, a number of church organizations and denominations around the world continue to give women freedom to lead in areas where they are most gifted. Question: Are they motivated by a critical lack of workers, or do they understand the horrible philosophical roots of the detractor arguments?

ENDNOTES

15 1 Co 14:34, (NIV).

16 Linda L. Belleville, Contributor, *Two Views on Women in Ministry*, (Zondervan Publishing House: Grand Rapids, Michigan, 2001), 77.

17 Stanley J. Grenz & Denise Muir Kjesbo, *Women in the Church: A Biblical Theology of Women in Ministry*,(Illinois:Inter Varsity Press, 1995), 14-15.

18 Beck & Blomberg, 16

19 Grenz & Kjesbo, 14-15.

20 Beck & Blomberg, 16.

21 Ibid.

22 Belleville, 78.

23 2 Pet. 3:16 (NIV).

24 Hermeneutics may be defined as that aspect of biblical study that deals with principles of interpretation – Tucker & Liefeld, 443

Chapter 4

How Culture and Tradition Impacts Argument

It was such a beautiful day. A cool breeze blew through the large open windows from the nearby ocean. It refreshed the hospital room where I was ministering to a patient at the San Fernando General Hospital.

Then, as if a sand storm had erupted, the scene turned ugly. A man I had never met rudely interrupted, rebuking me. He yelled that I was usurping a ministerial role that was not legitimate for a woman. I described this incident in Chapter One.

You can imagine how his anger rattled me. I immediately lost my train of thought. I felt completely embarrassed, intimidated and furious (in that order). I thought, "How terrible that, in rendering such an honorable service, I should be battered by a stranger yelling at me—and in a place where patients desperately needed spiritual counsel, and quiet!"

However, later on, when I had re-gathered my wits, I could tell that he was motivated, not for Biblical reasons, but cultural. He was an East Indian man. I recognized that this raving male held the traditional[25] and cultural view that women should be at home, hidden from the eyes of the public, and engaged in domestic affairs. From observation, East Indian women in Trinidad have not always been in the forefront. For the most part, their culture mandates that they live secluded lives, although this pattern has been changing rapidly over the years.[26] This is a custom, a cultural issue that has become a 'tradition.'[27]

Yet, that embarrassing experience remains firmly in my mind; it typifies the cultural argument against women in ministry with which I have repeatedly been accosted by pastors.

What do I mean by "cultural argument"?

Sir Edward Tylor, pioneer British anthropologist, defines 'culture' as "that complex whole which includes knowledge, belief, art, morals, law, custom, and any other capabilities and habits acquired by man as a member of society."[28]

Grunlan and Mayers, authors of "Cultural Anthropology," offer a more concise definition. They define 'culture' as "learned and shared attitudes, values, and ways of behaving."[29]

The East Indian culture is not something about which I am ignorant since I was born into it. Before my conversion I, like the typical young person of that culture, lived a sheltered life with no real reason to venture out into the public eye. This changed after I joined the church. The church women went out into the community and often went to the hospital to share the gospel with others. To evangelize the community was almost an unspoken requirement of the women. For this reason, when I joined the church, I actually entered another culture. I also embraced a new pattern of behavior, or role that mirrored my new 'status.'[30]

In retrospect, I think that the man who berated me at that bedside was acting on the assumption that public ministry was a role strictly reserved for a priest—who he felt should be a man; never a woman. Is he right? Are some ministering roles exclusively male and others female? If so, is this true of all cultures?

On this subject of roles, Grunlan and Mayers write, "Although biology limits certain roles only to women, such as giving birth and nursing infants, and others only to men, such as fathering children, **it is society that assigns most roles to one sex or the other"** (emphasis mine). What may be a male role in one society may be a female role in another."[31] Citing examples, they go on to say that "Blanket weaving is a male role in Hopi society but a female role in Navaho society. Hunting and fishing are predominantly male roles in most societies; but agricultural work is a female role in almost as many societies as it is a male role." [32]

Worldwide, the roles of women are as diverse as the traditions they uphold and the societies in which they live. It is not uncommon to find that within one region, e.g., the Mediterranean Basin, that the roles of women (Greek, Egyptian, Roman) may differ vastly as shown in subsequent paragraphs. I was startled to discover that in ancient Greece, vast cultural differences exist among women who live in the same country, but in separate cities, i.e., as Athens and Sparta as is subsequently revealed.

Also, in other societies, like the ancient Jewish community, women are treated as the worldview[33] of the religious leaders of that community regarding women would dictate. I look forward to sharing more on this with you later in this chapter.

Women in the Mediterranean World

In regard to this discussion, I was impressed how John Temple Bristow, author of *What Paul Really Said about Women*, presented the cultural diversity among women of the Mediterranean region who were contemporaries of the Apostle Paul.

Athenian Women

Bristow writes, "Respectable Athenian Greek wives led a completely secluded life,"[34] taking "no part in public affairs"[35] nor were they found together with their husbands "at social events like private dinner parties."[36] While their men "enjoyed outdoor sports and frequented the *agora,* the marketplace, which served as the centre of city life and communication" they were restricted in participating in recreational activities and had limited social contacts.[37] They "never went out alone, never shared meals with men, and never entered into the life of the community."[38] The few with a modest education were able to discuss current literature and philosophical thought.

Ironically, these women were, for the most part, upper-class prostitutes known as courtesans. These were the people men invited to attend lectures and enter into intellectual discussions and debates with their clients.[39]

Bristow reports that married couples carried on no conversations. Such social intercourse was "neither valued nor expected."[40] The ideal Athenian woman, as Bristow describes, is a woman who sees, hears, and inquires about as little as possible. She ideally remains secluded at home, hidden from the eyes of the public, continually engaged in domestic affairs.

Spartan Women

In contrast, Spartan women enjoyed a considerable number of freedoms, including economic, and even maintained political responsibilities. Bristow suggests a reason for all of the liberties of Spartan women. It has to do with the fact that in previous generations, they owned two-thirds of all the land.[41]

Egyptian Women

How different it was in Egypt. Unlike Athens, and even surpassing Sparta, the Egyptians showed incredible respect for women. They regularly visited local markets. They held many of the jobs in the trade crafts. In their culture, men tended to stay at home and handle the weaving. Basically, they enjoyed the same legal rights as the men of their same social class.[42] These women were not the least bit hesitant to appear in public, whether to shop (at the marketplace) or to support their husbands on the streets. In the first recorded labor strike, they stood on the picket line supporting the cause of their husbands.

As Barbara Lesko describes them, the Egyptian couple went everywhere together. This noted Egyptologist describes such married couples as enjoying respect and equality not only within their secular and religious communities, but also under the law as well.[43]

Roman Women

In Rome daughters were less valued and less favored than sons. However, Roman women still had educational opportunities, and generally enjoyed a great deal of freedom. Wives would often accompany their husbands to social occasions. Husbands considered them as supporting partners, and confidants. If the husband was a member of an upper class, his wife could get a professional education, and organize meetings.[44]

Jewish Women

The rights and roles of women in Israel, under the Rabbis, were much more complicated. Even the Rabbis couldn't agree on these issues for women. A minority argued that women should enjoy sexual equality. But the majority insisted on treating males as being superior. The result produced an ugly bias among fathers who considered a daughter as a trap.

One writer describes this lifetime of worry for each girl child as occurring from the cradle to the grave. During her adolescence he feared that she might be seduced. When she matured into a maiden – his concern shifted to issues of promiscuity. When she reached adulthood, his angst focused on getting her married. From the moment the wedding dress was put into the closet he began to concern himself about her bearing children. He even fretted over whether or not, in old age, she might turn to witchcraft.[45] No wonder some of them lamented, "Woe to man who has a daughter—she will be a trap for life!"

Thanks to the teaching of the rabbis, Jewish men felt it was inappropriate for them to even speak to a woman in public - including one's own wife. For a woman to speak to a man who was not her husband was seen as giving evidence that she had committed adultery with him, and could be divorced.

You can imagine the scandal Jesus caused when he regularly sought the company of women, conversed with them as with men, and even allowed prostitutes to talk to him and even pour perfume on his feet.

Contrast this with the first prayer by which every Jew began every new day; that every male Jew was required to recite:

> "O God, I thank you for not making me a Gentile... a woman... or a boor."

Where did such ideas come from?

Many Jewish historians are convinced that this unfortunate mindset stemmed from a misinterpretation of the tenth commandment, "You shall not covet your neighbor's wife. You shall not set your desire on your neighbor's house or land, his manservant or maidservant, his ox or donkey, or anything that belongs to your neighbor" (Deut 5:21).

Where did such erroneous Biblical interpretation begin? It started with the terrible idea of classifying a 'wife' as a possession, similar to one's house, land, servants, and animals.

Early Rabbinic interpretation assumed that wives were "owned" by their husbands. Such fuzzy thinking led many to treat their wives as 'objects' rather than equals.[46] Today Bible scholars agree that such interpretation is a grossly bad interpretation that ignores the context in which the commandment was given. Where did they get this despicable idea? History also shows that this thinking was influenced by the pagan cultures surrounding Israel.

Another contributing factor was the mistaken idea that women have stronger tendencies to sin than men. As a result, girls were discouraged from reading and studying the Torah even as every young boy was required to do so.[47] However, a few rabbis did encourage fathers to teach the Torah to their daughters.[48]

In the extreme, this corrupt exegesis produced Jewish extremists who promoted the idea of women as evil distractions. Ironically, while this extreme view was held by only a minority of Rabbis, still, it managed to move the entire rabbinical leadership to establish a hard and fast rule that no man should speak to a woman in public, even if she was his wife or daughter. Notice that the basis for this theological position was only a cultural idea!

As a result of this binding rule, a group of radicals emerged, called the "Bleeding Pharisees." What produced the blood? Embracing this foolish rule (as 'gospel'), they felt that to honor God, the only safe way to move among the public was by keeping ones eyes shut. Of course, such silly behavior will produce bruises, welts, and bleeding lacerations. Isn't it amazing that these zany people were willing to endure such pain to preserve a cultural position regarding women?

Even at congregational worship, Jewish women were segregated into a separate court in Herod's Temple. [49] Where did such an idea originate? Certainly not from the Old Testament; in its description of the Temple lay-out, such arrangements are conspicuously absent from the Biblical account.

To spread these nutty ideas to the entire known world, these Rabbis had the help of the leading Jewish philosopher, Philo of Alexandria. He was so anxious to promote any idea that would enable the Jewish community to survive amid a multi-cultural world dominated by Romans, that he thoroughly "Hellenized" them, i.e., caused them to be dominated by cultural ideas regarding the role of women in society and religion originated by the Greeks.

Yet, amazingly, in the broad Mediterranean world, cultural views of women varied. While many cultures considered women as chattel, there were exceptions. For example, in the Egyptian and Spartan cultures, women enjoyed egalitarian lifestyles without the restrictive seclusion that Athenian women endured.

Incidentally, while Philo was familiar with the freedom the Spartan and Egyptian women enjoyed, he chose to ignore it in order to promote his punishing cultural opinion. When asked why, he said that he considered such views irrelevant to the world he sought to foster by his writing. His attitude is evidence that this awful view of women dominated both the political as well as the philosophical fabric of the entire world. So, in my research, I was anxious to find out where all of this came from. I found insight from David Hamilton, co-author of *Why Not Women* that sheds some light.

Women Berated in Ancient Greece

Hamilton draws us back in time to a scene in ancient Greece where Plato, the great philosopher, was instructing young men about the facts of life:

> "There is no Hades. We have no fear of punishment in some desolate after place. Our punishment is with us, here and now. The price for our sinning was exacted at the beginning of time by Zeus himself when he afflicted us with *these creatures*. He also designed it so that we can neither exist without their aid nor bear their company! We cannot escape this pain, for it lives among us. It is *our sisters, our mothers, our betrothed, our wives and daughters, our mistresses and concubines.*[50].

Hamilton argues that if we want to understand the typical Western mindset about women and their roles we have to go back to the Greeks. It was teaching patterned such as described above that laid the foundations of belief for the Mediterranean world, the conquered lands of the Roman Empire, and finally, all of Western civilization.[51]

Is Hamilton right when he insists that in everything from best-selling books to the plots of movies at the local theater to what is taught in our universities, seminaries, and Bible schools, Plato and the Greek philosophers, poets, playwrights, physicians, and political thinkers continually seek to influence modern thinking? [52] The evidence points to a resounding "yes!" Still I wondered about where such ideas stemmed.

As I dug into this I finally found the headwaters of this polluted stream. To appreciate the evolution flowing from the ancient Greek world to the twenty first century, you need to keep in mind these stellar names: Socrates, Plato, Aristotle, Alexander, and Aquinas. Everything in print concerning the cultural view of women stems from the ideas of these teachers. Also, the order matters; it all begins with Socrates, the procreator of such ideas.

He is first because he discipled Plato, who, in turn shaped the thinking of his pupil, the brilliant Aristotle. Then Aristotle was hired by a father to tutor his son, who became known as Alexander the Great. As he conquered the known world, he unified its cultures by imposing Greek ideas. He "Hellenized these cultures". As a result in every capital city and educational institution the values and ideas of Greek culture were embraced. And why not—a superior civilization (with its superior gods) had conquered them; so it must have better ideas; therefore, why not buy into them. Such thinking pervaded not only the Roman world, but also the Jewish culture.

Still, I wanted to know what ideas had sparked the thinking of Socrates regarding women in the first place. In studying his personal history I discovered the reason. He, although married, practiced homosexuality. As a result, his lectures promoted the idea that promiscuous homosexuality was a "superior form of love."

His reasoning was based on two assumptions. First, he felt that homosexual love combined "the love of a beautiful body" with "the love of a beautiful soul." Second, he felt that women were inferior, which he calculated to be halfway between a man and an animal. Their main reason for being was to produce heirs.

Thanks to this man's perverted thinking educated and sophisticated members of the male Athenian population preferred to socialize with their own gender and sexually cavort with young boys. He shaped Plato, his prize pupil's thinking.

Through his writings, Plato promoted the idea that the only way a man could possibly appreciate the authentic beauty of nature was upon rising from his bed after a night of perverted philandering with a young boy. Plato wrote many poems and essays extolling this type of love-making. Many are wistful reflections on his encounters with males barely into puberty. Small wonder; there was no place in his world or in his personal life for women. All of this weirdness was to take a giant step forward through his star pupil, the brilliant Aristotle.

Did Aristotle embrace these same views? If you visit your local library you will discover them in an essay he wrote on the subject of how a queen bee would guide a huge swarm of bees to a new hive. In this treatise, titled "The Queen Bee", you will see how he stressed how they all worked in harmony to build a harmonious society. Unfortunately, Aristotle's subject (and title) was not "Queen Bee", but "*King Bee*!" The title it now has, "Queen Bee" was created by historical revisionists to mask the perversion he espoused in this piece, even among honey bees. His original idea of the hive being led by a "king bee" was based on the ideas taught him by Socrates and Plato, i.e., that the male is the naturally superior leader; while women, in his view, were considered naturally inferior.

The original manuscript based his choice of a King over a Queen bee on his viewpoint that the male species, in the natural realm, is better suited to lead, since he is a male. He then argued that women, by virtue of their inherent weakness, and inherent lack of courage are not meant to lead society, but only obey.

Such views espoused by Aristotle were spread like seeds by a tornado, all over the lands that his star pupil, Alexander the Great, conquered. They managed to promote homosexuality to the point that it became very popular, except among the Jewish culture.

They also convinced the conquered cultures to embrace the idea that women, being only sub-human (half animal), were not only unfit for education, but should be locked away by their husbands and made completely subservient. From sunny Greece all the way across the Mediterranean to India, these views changed and dominated thinking—even, in some respects—in Judea. So, from 300AD to the twenty-first century, such Hellenized thinking has controlled the destinies of women. I bear witness that it is alive and well in Trinidad.

The question arises: if the Jews did not embrace homosexuality (and they adamantly opposed it) what parts of Socrates-Plato-Aristotle's ideas did they buy into? As you can surmise from only what we have discussed earlier in this chapter, the demeaning inferiority of women promoted by the rabbinic leaders came directly from Socrates.

As Christianity came into existence through the teaching of Jesus, and then the apostles, this maltreatment of women was abated. Both embraced the idea of the equality of women and each reached out to embrace the use of their gifts in areas of ministry and leadership. But about two generations later, as a result of the Hellenization and the strong Pharisaical influence, many Christian writers reverted to the old views of women, seeing them in the Socratic viewpoint. They even imposed such views on the writing of Paul, assuming that he shared this "Hellenized" Socratic viewpoint.

Is it not amazing how a perspective can infect entire countries and cultures, and exert so much influence without people ever understanding its roots, or how their worldview was colored by it? How did the ideas of Socrates become so pervasive in the modern day?

With the decline of the Roman world, the views of Aristotle were lost for centuries; then came the historical period known as the Enlightenment. During this era, 1300 years after the Pauline Epistles were written, a Christian scholar, Thomas Aquinas, rediscovered these Aristotelian ideas about women and wrote about them. As a result they became woven into his ideas of Christian ministry, influencing both the Roman Catholic Church as well as its Protestant counterpart. Next to Augustine's, the views of Aquinas' ideas still dominate much church thinking. It is from his interpretation of the words of Paul regarding women in ministry that the Roman Catholic Church and even my Detractors get their ideas regarding female ministry.

If one reads Paul with the viewpoint of Aristotle, just as Aquinas did, without seeking to analyze the meaning of his words, one might conclude that his interpretation, together with those of most Church Fathers and Reformers, were right.

However, when you carefully and accurately examine the key writings of Paul on women in ministry, you discover that he vehemently opposed such ideas, even though he wrote against a cultural matrix dominated by a cult that elevated women to prominence by making worship a function of prostitution. This we will do with precision and thoroughness in the two succeeding chapters.

You are about to discover insights free of the cultural baggage of Socratic thinking. Once and for all, you will discover the true interpretation of the Biblical verses my Detractors have used like machetes. Thank God that the perverted views of Plato and his ilk can not hide from the glaring light of sound exegesis.

ENDNOTES

25 'Traditionalist' is the term given to one category of believers who place restrictions on women's roles in the church.
26 The writer has been residing in Trinidad from birth for over forty years.
27 Webster defines tradition as the handing down of information, beliefs, and customs by word of mouth or by example from one generation to another without written instruction.
28 Edward Tylor, Quoted in Stephen A. Grunlan and Marvin K. Mayers, *Cultural Anthropology: A Christian Perspective*, (Zondervan Publishing House, January, 1979), 41.
29 Stephen A. Grunlan and Marvin K Mayers., *Cultural Anthropology: A Christian Perspective* (Eugene, Oregon: Zondervan, 1979), 41.
30 Grunlan and Mayers define *status* as a "position or place in a social system and its attendant rights and duties," 135
31 Ibid. , 137.
32 Ibid. , 137-138.
33 Worldview is a community's view of reality, the largely implicit assumptions that underlie a culture.
34 John Temple Bristow, *What Paul Really Said About Women: An Apostle's Liberating Views On Equality In Marriage, Leadership, and Love* (New York: HarperCollins Publishers, 1991), 5.
35 Ibid.
36 Barbara S. Lesko, *The Remarkable Women of Ancient Egypt* (Berkeley: B.C. Scribe Publications, 1978), 30-31; Quoted in Bristow, *What Paul Really Said About Women*, 11.
37 Bristow, 5.
38 Ibid. , 7-8.
39 Ibid. , 8.
40 Ibid, 5.
41 Ibid. , 9.
42 Ibid. , 10.
43 Lesko, 11.
44 Bristow, 12.
45 45 B. Sanhedrin 100b. Quoted in Rachel Biale, *Women and Jewish Law:An Exploration of Women's Issues in Halakhic Sources* (New York: Schocken Books, 1984), 275-276, and note 13. Quoted in Cunningham & Hamilton, 103.
46 Cunningham & Hamilton, 104.
47 Ibid. , 106.
48 Ibid.
49 Ibid. , 105.
50 Ibid. , 72.
51 Ibid. , 72-73.
52 Ibid.

Chapter 5

Showdown in Corinth

Analysis of I Corinthians 11:2-16 and 14:26-40

Jeremiah Johnson was a mid-westerner who decided to become a man living in the wilderness of the Rockies in the USA. On one occasion, he killed an Indian warrior defending himself in a fair fight.

However, the Tribe to which this Indian belonged declared war on Johnson. For nearly a decade, the Tribe would choose a male to jump him while he slept, or hunkered down in the rain and blizzard.

He never knew when, or from where his next attacker would charge at him. He lived a nightmare existence until the Tribe declared him vindicated.

I feel like this Mountain Man. Repeatedly attackers have "jumped" me! Inevitably, every encounter turns to a debate over four key Scriptural passages, all written by Paul.

Each of these Biblical passages contains "catch phrases" that my Detractors are convinced provide sufficient proof to warrant me announcing my resignation from the pulpit.

Two of these passages occur in this Corinthian passage spanning Chapters 11 through 14, the issues of "headship" and "women keep silent", which I shall deal with now. These chapters make up a major section in which Paul counsels the believers on the purpose of worship, edification, and how leaders are to function to produce edifying worship.

To enable you to have a clear picture of the meaning of each of these passages, we offer this simple outline to help you track our discussion:

1. Women and the Corinthian Culture
2. The Headship Debate (1 Cor. 11:2-16)
3. The "Keep Silent" Debate (1 Cor. 14:26-40)
4. Summary: What All this Means

As we learned in Chapter Three, proper exegetical analysis requires us to first examine the cultural context as it existed in Corinth.

1. Women and the Corinthian Culture

Corinth was a port city, strategically located on a major crossroads in that area of Greece. It was a bustling hub of worldwide commerce. It was also a city of social, cultural, and religious diversity.

Corinth was also a renowned religious center. Shrines and temples dominated the skyline, the most prominent among them being the Temple of Aphrodite. Aphrodite was the Greek goddess of erotic love. She was worshipped throughout the Mediterranean world and especially in Corinth.[53] As a result, prostitution, drunkenness, sexual promiscuity, and corruption were the order of the day.[54] To give this lifestyle a rationale, the people turned to a philosophy with religious overtones, called Gnosticism. This "religion" dominated the thinking of Corinthians.

The Corinthian Church, founded by Paul in about the year A.D. 50, was in no way free of the problems plaguing the society at large. While Paul was at Ephesus, during his third missionary journey, he received verbal and written reports of the problems, pressures and struggles, of a church called out of a pagan society.[55] He learned that on the spiritual front, Corinth was plagued with false teachings and the false cultic practices of Gnosticism had made in-roads. To appreciate how this evil religion could gain a foot-hold in that church we must understand that its core beliefs stemmed from a perversion of Scriptures, particularly the early chapters of Genesis as well as other parts of the Old Testament, including these tenets:

- It taught that matter is evil.

- It viewed the God of the Bible as an 'inferior' deity because of His creation of the physical world; and the physical realm was considered inferior to the spiritual realm.
- It contended that Eve enjoys an exalted position as the mother goddess, who gave birth to Yahweh and Elohim. Gnostics believed that she was the source of all life, since she gave birth to Adam and brought knowledge to man.
- This cult emphasized the concept of 'spiritual enlightenment', which they contended could only be learned from women. Among their stranger ideas was the concept that motherhood was exalted, but child bearing was considered sinful.

Unfortunately, people converted from such beliefs to the Christian faith often managed to retain remnants of such Gnostic ideas creating doctrinal errors and dysfunctional thinking.

First Corinthians begins with Paul responding to many questions raised by the congregation. However, as he concludes the Epistle (and answered their questions), he raises issues critical to the health of the Body. In chapters 11 through 14, he brings up the subject of the true purpose for worship, and how all leaders, male and female—must lead the group in prayer and prophetic words to achieve the goal of edification.

Within the section dealing with worship, Paul points out the purpose for worship (edification) and the hindrances (improper use of Tongues, wrong use of Prophecy, and the improper conduct of leaders), with special words for women in leadership regarding Headship and Silence issues. These topics were bound to arise, since the Corinthian culture had produced such an interesting mix of women in attendance at worship service.

First, there were Godly women to be sure.

Second, there were bossy wives, no doubt, somewhat influenced by Gnosticism, exhibiting "know-it-all" attitudes and attempting to create disorder in the worship service. Such conditions will surprise no one familiar with the Corinthian culture, which encouraged women to participate in government debates that openly challenged all male opinions (including those of their husbands). As a result, the church must have often been tossed into disorder and confusion by the noisy female exchanges during worship.

Third, there were also former worshippers of Aphrodite, Dionysius, and other attendant goddesses in this pagan religion of Corinth.

Fourth, there were the aristocratic women from Rome whose cultural roots encouraged them to flaunt their wealth by wearing fashionable clothes, and sporting hairstyles and jewelry.

Fifth, the congregation must have included women delivered from slavery and prostitution.

Finally, you would see Greek and Jewish women emerging from suppressed seclusion. Certainly while the group is diverse, they shared one thing in common, a profound lack of education.

Some mix of people; sitting under one roof: a multi-racial, multi-cultural, multi-social, and multi-religious mix of women, all gifted, and seeking outlet for the expression of same. Add to this the fact of inexperienced leadership and you have a recipe for disorder and confusion. Yet, it was to this group that Paul shared very rich insights regarding edifying worship and the contribution and potential problems that women can experience in leading it.

To guide your thinking, we shall provide an in-depth exegetical analysis of each of the critical passages. In Section One, we shall take up Paul's counsel in 1 Cor. Eleven. The second Section will address his instructions and insight in 1 Cor. Fourteen.

2. Part One: Exegetical Analysis of 1 Cor. 11:2-16

A. Headship Issue

The concept of headship, as we understand it today (boss, leader, authority, ruler), does not find expression in Scripture except when reference is made to the secular rulers of Paul's day. Our use of the word 'head' denotes authority, dominion, or rule.

The Greeks' employment of the word 'head' differs greatly with our concept of 'chain of command' leadership popular today in business management as we think of a CEO as the 'head' of a corporation. The Greek word for "head" is *kephale. Kephale* is used to refer to the physical "head" as well as "source" or "origin" but not "ruler" or "leader."

The word for "ruler" or "leader" in the Hebrew is *ro'sh*. However, in 1 Corinthians 11:3 Paul used *kephale* in the Septuagint (the Greek translation of the Hebrew Scriptures) instead of *ro'sh*. The Greek's use of the word *kephale* conveys the idea of "source" or "origin."

The early Church Fathers were not ignorant of the Greek's use of the term "head". Cyril of Alexandria, fifth century Church Father, in commenting on 1 Cor. 11:3, wrote, "Thus we say that the *kephale* of every man is Christ, because he was made through Him and brought forward to birth. . . . And the *kephale* of woman is man, because she was taken from his flesh and has him as her source. Likewise, the *kephale* of Christ is God, because He is from Him according to nature." [56]

Paul raised this discussion about women in ministry because it touched cultural tradition, as the opening words of this chapter proclaim: *I commend you because you remember me in everything and maintain the traditions even as I have delivered them to you* (1 Cor. 11:2).

The tradition he has in mind is the one passed down from Adam, known as "headship", which describes a succession of hierarchy of functions involving the Father, Jesus, man, and woman.

The term "Headship" describes how power and responsibilities are to be distributed for maximum effectiveness. While all members of the Godhead and human family share different roles and responsibilities, they all share in common the attitude of a servant. This capability enables them to follow, as well as lead, in a manner that creates unity and an optimal effectiveness. We call this concept of leadership, Servant Leadership. It was designed to ensure that every person in the hierarchy could contribute to the success of the execution of the Divine Plan of saving and discipling people to full maturity as Sons of God. Paul describes it this way: "*. . . the head of every man is Christ, the head of a woman is her husband, and the head of Christ is God (Father)*" (1 Cor. 11:3).

Paul uses this concept of headship in two ways. First he wants to establish areas in which each member of the human and Divine family can function. The second use of head is as a metaphor.

As a metaphor for leadership, a human head sits on top the neck. Inside the skull are many nerves and organs, including the brain, eyes, ears, nose and mouth as well as a nervous and blood system capable of controlling the entire human anatomy. Therefore the metaphor works because it uses the picture of the human head running the human body, as a metaphor for spiritual leadership, i.e., the "head", running the body, i.e., setting priorities, determining direction, planning, supplying resources vital to the operation and growth—all the things that any organizational head would be responsible for making sure get accomplished.

Unfortunately, the Corinthian believers were not big on giving up control, so the concept of Headship that Paul presented would be a struggle for them to accept. Anticipating this, Paul surrounded this metaphor with two other examples of headship so all readers (then and now) of this Epistle could not miss his intended meaning for using the metaphor of "headship".

Metaphor # 1: The Head of Every Man is Christ

The first use of the metaphor, "the head of every man is Christ", asserts Christ's right to assume responsibility to fulfill the Father's will for a family of children with the nature of His own Beloved Son by redeeming and regenerating them and then placing His own nature within their spirits in order to live His life through them to enable them to mature into Christ-likeness (Col. 1:27).

True, some men are not fully aware of it, and many others reject the idea, but nevertheless, Jesus is their head, and they are responsible to follow Him. That is the whole objective of life for any man who wishes to fulfill his manhood. Of course, that is only seen in practice in the believer, and then only to a limited degree; but it is stated very positively here. Therefore, this metaphor means that Christ as *head* leads all of humankind by determining every man's eternal destiny.

Now, permit me to skip down to the third metaphor. Shortly, the reason will become clear.

Metaphor #3: Head of Christ is God

Paul describes this third level of headship mentioned here as, "the head of Christ is God." Jesus, the Son of God, equal with the Father in deity, nevertheless, demonstrated in history that he yielded to the practice of headship by always subordinating himself to the will of the Father. As a result, every minute of His life, He could truthfully say, "I do always those things which please my Father." This subordination is seen in His statement, "My Father is greater than I," (John 14:28).

Think about it—although equal with God, yet by becoming a man, Christ voluntarily consented to take a subordinate position to the Father. This is what He means when He said, "My Father is greater than I."

Now to the metaphor that the Corinthians struggled with—Metaphor #2.

Metaphor #2: Head of Woman is Man

Those first two headships help us to understand the meaning of this one; it is absolutely central to our discussion of the metaphor, "the head of the woman is the man." Actually the correct translation should be, "the head of the woman is the male". In understanding the meaning, we have two choices, since the word stood for a specific male human being, and also it could mean husband, i.e. the male of the marriage partnership. Clearly, the meaning cannot be the first one, since it would mean that the head of all women is a single male.

No, the only true interpretation is that Paul intended for the word, *aner,* to express the principle of men and women function in the marriage relationship. He meant that in terms of the marriage relationship there is a hierarchy of function, involving the subordination of the wife to the husband's leadership, which he viewed as similar to that described in Philippians 2 where the Son subordinated himself to the Father's will. Notice that subordination was not intended to be the same thing as domination. In the Philippian passage, you see that Christ balanced equality with subordination without ever descending into domination.

What made it work? His subordination was a voluntary commitment, carried out in pursuit of a mutual plan and shared conviction that God's will could best be achieved by this means. Likewise, a woman's subordination is voluntary; she joins the initiating leadership of her husband in building their marriage partnership to fulfill goals both agree upon, and commit to contribute toward.

So as we apply this concept to 1 Cor. 11:3, the concept that "the head of every woman is man" the entire verse shows that Paul is applying this universal principle of subordination in two ways:

- marriage relationships and,
- church (leadership) relationships

We will look at the first one briefly; but the second one we will analyze in depth because it is central to the issue of women in leadership, and relevant to the "covering" issue.

Headship and Marriage

When this principle of headship is applied to a marital relationship, the woman, by exchanging marriage vows, voluntarily takes this subordinate position. In this she grants to him the role of leader; and pledges that she will assume a supporting role to help him fulfill the objectives of their life together as Christ, his head, reveals it. Marriage means that the woman desires to help advance the objectives and goals of her husband. He becomes, therefore, the leader of the two. Paul has stated this aspect of headship very clearly.

Keep in mind that the key to submission has to do with the direction of their marriage, not about who rules and who follows. As they discuss the next step in their marriage relationship, the Lord provides the direction they should take. They reach consensus, because the man can show evidence of the Lord's answer to his prayer for direction, and because the woman subordinates her will to that same God given plan. Believe it, that process works in the congregation I lead, which is the other reason Paul raised this issue.

Headship and Church Relationships

The Corinthian church existed within the Eastern culture of the first century. So how were men and women to relate to each other, especially as they shared leadership?

In 1 Cor. 11:4 (and following) Paul applies this principle to the practice of the church, especially as it was lived within that culture, by saying:

> "Any man who prays or prophesies with his head covered dishonors his head, but any woman who prays or prophesies with her head unveiled dishonors her head—it is the same as if her head were shaven. For if a woman will not cover her head, then she should cut off her hair. But

since it is disgraceful for a woman to cut off her hair or shave her head, let her cover her head." (1 Corinthians 11:4-6 ESV).

Two things are very important to notice in these verses:

1. The center of Paul's concern is the public ministry of the Word of God.
2. He is talking here about Christians, about the church, the gathering of believers together in a public assembly.

The issues were not about whether a woman had the right to minister in public by teaching or preaching or leading in prayer in a church gathering attended by men; she did have that right. Rather, the issue was, when a woman functioned in a leadership capacity, how she should conduct herself so as to always demonstrate respect for the males (including, perhaps her husband) and her relationship to males (*aner*) in attendance as dictated by tradition of the Eastern culture within which she lived. In Corinth, that subordination was symbolized by her wearing a veil that completely covered her hair.

To appreciate the cultural pressure imposed on women in Corinth, consider what the veil meant to its citizens. If a woman ventured into public without a covering, she dishonored her husband, i.e., her head. Not wearing the veil also signified that a woman was a temple prostitute of the pagan cult that dominated the city. This gesture was her way of signaling her availability for sexual favors.

Therefore, the wearing of the veil was not an option if one were a loyal wife, or a moral single female. Any woman who appeared in public without a veil was opening herself up to the suspicion that she was worthy of the shame and disgrace public morals attached to her. So the wearing of the veil was not an option if one were a loyal wife, or a moral single female.

Therefore, you can imagine how disgraceful it would be for a woman to minister the Word in a Christian assembly, without that sign of acknowledgment of the principle of headship in her life. By wearing the veil as she exercised her prophetic (preaching) gifts she was acknowledging that she willingly abided by the principle of the headship in relationship to her own marriage as well as to the corporate direction of the church, achieved by consensus among all leaders.

I whole-heartedly agree to this principle in regard to church leadership matters. I insist that the direction of the congregation that I lead be determined by prayer and fasting among all leaders, both male and female.

As the Lord's next step of progress is revealed to us, I subordinate my will to that of the leadership. In this, I "wear the veil" to show my subordination with the will determined by and expressed through all our leadership.

So, I, in practicing this kind of leadership am, in fact, bringing my own female leadership into conformity with Paul's counsel regarding headship. Becoming a servant-leader enables me to minister, "wearing the veil".

Ironically, these same words were also used by Paul to advise male ministry leaders on how they must also conform to local cultural mandates. In Corinth, a man must never be seen in public (church auditorium or street corner) with his head covering. Therefore, Paul advises him to not dishonor his head (which is Christ) by wearing a hat or any article of clothing designed to cover one's head.

Paul's counsel is most remarkable because it contradicts the culture in which he was born and raised. The Jewish male never prays or spoke on the Word without a head covering, preferably a hat, but at least a yarmulke. This remains true today in Jewish worship services, and in every-day dress by orthodox sects, including the Hassid.

To me, Paul's counsel proves that he was being guided by the Holy Spirit, and not his own cultural prejudices. Truly, this suggests Divine revelation, does it not?

Summary

So let us return to the confrontation episode where my Detractors insisted that I cannot legitimately assume the role of a Pastor since I could never speak to males, because I was subordinate to their headship.

In light of what you now know, via careful analysis of what the headship issue was all about in 1Cor. 11, this passage does not forbid women from freely exercising ministry?

No, the issue was not if a woman could minister the Word but **how** she must go about it in order not to violate cultural rules. This is the central emphasis of this text: there is an approach to ministry that is appropriate for men, and another one for women. One is not better than the other; they are just different.

Paul next deals with how each gender must approach the task of ministry. For this discussion we will need to return to the passage we are analyzing. I will first share the English translation and then compare it to the original text that came from Paul's pen. It reads, *"If it is disgraceful for a woman to be shorn or shaven, let her wear a veil."* The very first word, by being poorly translated, creates a theological nightmare.

Notice the word "if". It should be translated as "since". Paul is connecting the matter of headship with wearing a veil. His point is: wherever local culture dictates that the absence of a veil is considered disgraceful, (i.e. in Corinth), then if a female ministry leader refuses to wear the sign of a relationship under headship, she is making it known that she rejects all headship (including Christ's). This would surely disqualify her from ministry.

However, Paul is also saying this: wherever the veil is not part of a culture, it will find another way of symbolizing the headship of a man over a woman, since the principle is universal. Therefore, a woman called to ministry leadership must make sure that she avails herself of the appropriate accessory that will show she honors and complies with the local culture. No matter what specific accessory a culture might dictate, including the wearing of a wedding ring to show her marital status, there is one universal thing that must dominate her dress and demeanor: modesty. (Its universality will become clear when you realize the source on which Paul bases his counsel).

The woman in ministry shows her respect for the God-ordained Headship by dressing modestly, and according to the manner appropriate for her gender. If married, she should wear a modest, but distinctly feminine wedding ring. She should also accessorize her apparel to reflect her modest attitude.

This is a profound teaching. It deserves an explanation, which the Apostle will now reveal as an introduction to the heart of this passage.

He tells us why this principle is true by showing where it began. It was mandated in the Garden of Eden:

> "For a man ought not to cover his head, since he is the image and glory of God; but woman is the glory of man. For man was not made from woman, but woman from man. Neither was man created for woman, but woman for man." (1 Corinthians 11:7-9 ESV).

Notice that Paul does not base his reason on any local custom. He returns to the Garden of Eden in order to find a basis that will make this principle universally applicable to all women in ministry leadership. His point:

this principle of "Headship" must be embraced by women in ministry leadership because it has existed from the beginning of mankind.

Genesis reveals that man was made in the image and glory of God. This word, translated as "Image", means that something is being manifested; something that was invisible is suddenly made visible. In this case it is God's own nature. Man was made in God's image in order that any creature, looking at a man, would see the likeness, the very nature of God. That is the dignity of humanity.

Notice also, that this statement removes the principle from being reduced to a "male vs. female" issue, since this principle was declared before the two sexes were ever separated. So this timing shows that this headship is first and foremost a way of demonstrating the truth that both genders equally share this same image. To prove this point, Paul adds,

"God created them in the beginning male and female and He named them **Adam"** (Gen. 5:1).

Notice that this word, Adam, is singular. The purpose for its use was to show that the female gender shares equally with her male counterpart in fully reflecting the true image and glory of God. Otherwise He would have named them "Adams".

So where are their roles different? The answer to this most important question lies in understanding the meaning of the Hebrew word for "glory". The meaning implies that in which one takes delight. Think about it—man's creation reflects the nature of God and in that God takes great delight in the way man reflects His glory. Now let's translate this analysis into the Corinthian situation.

For this reason, Paul asserts, in Corinth, God is publicly and openly manifested when the man does not wear a veil, i.e., to cover God's creative glory. He is to be unveiled so that the glory of God in creation should be visibly manifest to everyone.

This manifestation was first modeled by Jesus; it was in reflecting the glory of the Father (headship) that people in crowds are drawn to God. In Jesus, people caught a glimpse of the glory and delight that God takes in humanity. This insight triggered a longing (in their hearts) to find the way back to the enjoyment of that delight. This is the very thing that John is driving at in the introduction to his Gospel when he writes, "the Word became flesh and dwelt among us," and "we beheld his glory," (John 1:14).

This is the glory that a man, a male, is called upon to manifest in the ministry of the Word. He is not to be veiled because he is proclaiming that open delight which God takes in the creation of mankind. In so complying, man is demonstrating that he is also under a headship—to the Lord Jesus. So, in the final analysis, both men in ministry and their female counterparts are both under headships.

Similarly, since woman is the glory of the man, it is *in her* that the man finds his delight. Woman is the delight of man. But man only discovers this in the joys of marital intimacy. It was not meant to be showcased to the public. Therefore, the veil symbolizes this kind of intimacy that only two people within the marriage bond can experience.

Thus, in relation to marriage, the veil is not a mark of subjection, but a mark of intimacy, i.e., of a marital privacy voluntarily assumed by a woman. She is not forced to give herself to the man, she deliberately chooses to do so, but from then on she is marked out as belonging to him.

In our modern world, as was mentioned, the wedding ring serves as an equivalent of the veil, since it marks a woman as belonging to another, already claimed. She has given herself freely and voluntarily to a man; she has already surrendered her right to herself to him.

Today, in the Eastern world, the veil still symbolizes that the woman wearing it is not selling sexual favors or condoning promiscuity. All of her physical intimacy belongs exclusively to no one but her husband (who, in turn, wholly belongs to her).

She is also reflecting another aspect of glory—the special delight that accompanies the experience of being redeemed. In this way the intimacy of marriage becomes a metaphor to reflect the ecstasy one experiences when one becomes redeemed—experiencing the extraordinary and intimate love relationship of a bride with her bridegroom on their wedding night.

Therefore, in wearing the veil, the woman is bearing testimony of the special delight which Christ enjoys with His redeemed people. This is why woman was created:

> "For man was not made from woman, but woman from man. Neither was man created for woman, but woman for man." (1 Cor.11:8)

Again, notice the phrase, "…for him…". It suggests that the woman was separated and brought to man that she might be 'for' him. This, I think, is the key thought involved in headship. She is *for* her husband, i.e., behind him, backing him up; supportive of him. She wants him to succeed and she is deeply involved in the process, undergirding him in every way she can, and finding delight in doing so. And what is the purpose of this? It is all designed so that, together, they might achieve the objectives which his head, Christ, has set before them.

A woman's subordination in the marriage relationship demonstrates that she honors Christ, and the universality of this Divinely established principle.

Then as she functions in ministry leadership, she uses her power (modesty and voluntary subordination) to facilitate the kind of order that fosters edifying worship. He then touches on the connection between her expression of headship, the resulting creation of order, and the pleasing of the angels who love order and obey the law of headship by expressing their subordination to Christ by covering their faces when they worship at His Throne, as Paul points out in 1 Cor. 11:10: *"That is why a woman ought to have a symbol of authority on her head, because of the angels"*. Paul's point in introducing angels in regard to headship is because angels are always concerned about preserving the worship of humans from any practice that would deny the God ordained distinctive which the sexes are to manifest to each other, and to society at large.

Having made a strong case for the distinctions between the sexes, Paul now balances this with a powerful statement of the equality of men and women in marriage.

> "Nevertheless, in the Lord woman is not independent of man nor man of woman; for as woman was made from man, so man is now born of woman. And all things are from God" (1 Corinthians 11:11-12).

Here is a very positive statement of the full equality (as persons) of men and women. Absolutely no inferiority of one sex to the other is implied. How different from the lies perpetrated on the Western world by Socrates and his ilk, insisting that the inferiority of women is natural and appropriate.

In stark contrast, Paul asserts that in Christ's redemption, the original intent of God is restored. Both genders are equal as persons, yet each is distinct, functioning in a divinely given order which is to be freely accepted by the woman so as to demonstrate to the watching world her delight with the order God has established throughout creation.

By obeying the Headship principle, a woman, both in marriage and in ministerial leadership, restores her legitimate right to exercise her spiritual gifts and calling in prophetic ministry.

Finally, Paul states, that if one objectively and honestly observes the implications of this principle of headship from nature, one will find its rightness validated:

> "Judge for yourselves; is it proper for a woman to pray to God with her head uncovered? Does not nature itself teach you that for a man to wear long hair is degrading to him, but if a woman has long hair, it is her pride? For her hair is given to her for a covering" (1 Cor. 11:13-15).

This is really a second argument the apostle gives to support the matter of wearing a veil.

(The first argument: obeying the cultural mandate demonstrates compliance with the headship principle, thereby establishing her rightful authority to speak the Word authoritatively which the prophetic ministry requires).

Geneticists tell us that it takes two genes in a woman to produce baldness, but only one in a man. Some women do get bald, but it is very rare. While a young man can get away with long hair, an older man cannot. It degrades him, i.e., diminishes his credibility as a spiritual leader.

On the other hand, while an older woman can lose her complexion to wrinkles and her youthful figure to gravity, still, in old age, she can have beautiful hair. Paul argues that nature demonstrates that she was given more beautiful hair than men in order to manifest the principle of headship. In fact, in a culture where the wearing of veils is not a custom, then her long hair (longer than her husband's) could serve as an adequate expression of her commitment to the principle of headship.

However, because in the Roman world, especially in Corinth, where veil-wearing was still the custom, Paul concludes the passage with these words:

> "If any one is disposed to be contentious, we recognize no other practice, nor do the churches of God" (1 Corinthians 11:16).

Paul concludes by saying, "There is no need to argue the point since the headship principle is so widely understood in all of the Pauline churches that if a woman attempted to exercise ministry leadership without wearing the veil, since it is culturally appropriate to do so, the congregation and leadership would take disciplinary action.

Surely, from this passage any accusation that a woman is disqualified from vocational ministry because she lacks a covering other than the one that is the subject of this passage of Scripture is absurd.

Concluding Remarks on Headship

As we have seen, promoters of the idea that women ought not to do anything in the kingdom without the approval of a man and submission to his authority, has felt comfortable that they had 1 Cor. 11:2-16 to support their ideas.

In the passage we have learned two important truths relative to our issue.

First, we learned that both men and women were permitted to use their Word gifts to perform a prophetic ministry in the Corinthian congregation. So let us briefly revisit the discussion on 1Cor. 11:4, 5, "Every man praying or prophesying . . ." and ". . . every woman who prays or prophesies . . ." Notice that this passage clearly affirms that women, as well as men, belong in pastoral leadership.

In light of the prevailing philosophies regarding women of the Jewish community, in which Paul had been born and raised, I find it amazing that he would so strenuously advocate the right of women to share ministry leadership positions in the congregation. Nevertheless, for women, Paul did impose restrictions that had been dictated by cultural issues, which led to the second thing that Biblical passage revealed.

Second, we learned that while women were included in praying and preaching they must adhere to the rules of the culture that dominated Corinth, which required women to dress appropriately, wearing the head covering, and men to dress appropriately, by not wearing one. For women, the wearing of a head covering demonstrated that they recognized God's moral order of leadership that extended from God through both human genders. If a woman should violate the cultural rules of wearing a veil, it would send a signal to the watching world that she might be a prostitute; it would mark her with shame. As a result of some female preachers' disregard for this cultural mandate non-Christians in the city were laughing at the Church and rejecting the Gospel it proclaimed.

The passage makes this important point regarding women in ministry: do not create confusion. In the next passage (1 Cor. 14) the focus will be on them not to create disorder.

However, as you now know, by using the rules of Expositional Hermeneutics we have achieved clarity that robs these advocates of a Biblical "weapon". The fact is that a woman, whether a wife or a Pastor, can honor the universal principle set down in the Garden of Eden, and still fulfill a calling to prophetic ministry leadership. The text will permit no other conclusion.

Section Two: Analysis of the other Corinthian Passage (1 Cor. 14:26-40)

B. Keep Silent Issue

"Lady, how can you Pastor when the Bible says that women must subordinate themselves to male leadership?"

This, as you know by now, is the "Headship Issue". It is the first of four Biblical arguments that my Detractors have aimed at me with intent to kill my ministry.

Having settled that argument, I am eager now to move on to deal with the second reason my Detractors have used to dissuade me from fulfilling my calling: "Lady, how can you preach when the Bible says, "women are to keep silent?"

This issue understandably arose in a New Testament church steeped in the culture that promoted the idea of women occupying prominent roles in society, whether in the cultic worship already described, or in the world of politics, by publicly participating in civic affairs.

Truly, the cultural shadow produced a legitimate concern for how women should conduct themselves in public worship. The evidence shows that certain females were disrupting the worship service by their social chattering and shouting questions to their husbands seated elsewhere during worship.

Therefore Paul proposed a solution: stop the "chit-chat" and "save your questions until you get home". He summarized this counsel in the phrase, "...let the women keep silent in the church..." I am as familiar with this phrase as the back of my hands, since I have had it leveled at me like a loaded weapon. If I had a dollar for every time I had this Biblical verse thrown at me, I could pay off a credit card.

Fortunately, there is a clear explanation of what Paul intended this phrase to mean which can be realized by using the laws of Hermeneutics and the tools of exegetical research. To this end, we will proceed by first examining the context in which the phrase occurs, and then studying the meaning of the key words in the language in which they were written since, if one relies only on the English translation, the phrase does tend to support the argument of my Detractors.

At the outset of our investigation, we should show how this counsel of Paul relates to that given in 1 Cor. Chapter 11. Recall that in that passage we discovered that it is important that the headship issue is resolved to avoid creating confusion. In Chapter 14 we shall learn that the silence issue must be resolved to avoid disorder. To appreciate this we will now nail down the exegetical basis for what we have been saying all along in this chapter regarding the purpose of worship being edification. We take up the Biblical analysis at this point (rather than earlier) because it is specifically stated in this passage.

Purpose of Worship

Paul's ideal meeting in the early church had this as its primary objective, "Let all things be done for edification" (1 Cor. 14:26). This word translated as "edification", is the Greek word, *oikedome.* It is comprised of two words, *oike* meaning 'house' and the word *demo* meaning 'to construct'. By conjoining these two words we have the Greek word which means "to build up". Incidentally, this word is always used in connection with building up people, (i.e. not building physical structures).

Edification becomes the objective of an ideal worship experience because it results in these benefits: hearts are uplifted and heads are encouraged and the assembled people enjoy an expectancy that God is going to meet them and affirm, by His Presence, that He will accompany them through their week and share their burdens. As you can imagine, Paul wanted this to be the priority of all who exercised their gifts in public ministry.

1 Cor.14:26-40 examines three problems which can wreck the edifying process in worship. They included the wrong use of Tongues; the wrong use of Prophesying; and the wrong idea regarding women ministering in the service. To abuse the proper use of Tongues and Prophecy is to court the destruction of the edification process. However, since we desire to stay on subject, we will bypass the opportunity to discuss these two problems, and deal only with the third: potential danger to edifying fellowship—the involvement of women in leadership who conduct themselves inappropriately. Therefore, out of this entire section spanning 1 Cor. 14:26 through 40, we shall only focus on 14: 34-38 since these verses directly relate to our debate.

Paul's mandate to the women in leadership was: conduct yourselves in a way that leads to edification; i.e., knowing when to speak and when to keep silent in church. In this context, he then discusses the hindrances that can thwart a woman's effectiveness in exercising pastoral leadership by preaching the Word.

How Women Leaders Hinder Edifying Worship

In spite of all the privileges enjoyed by women in the Corinthian congregation, problems arose. We encounter Paul's counsel related to this problem in 14:33-35:

> "For God is not the author of confusion but of peace, as in all the churches of the saints. Let your **women** keep **silent** in the churches, for they are not permitted to **speak**; but they are to be **submissive**, as the law also says. And if they want to learn something, let them ask their own husbands at home; for it is shameful for women to speak in church." (1Cor. 14:33-35, NKJV, emphasis mine)

You cannot believe the people who, in reading this, want to write off Paul as a bachelor who hates women. In this passage, Paul will first describe the nature of the confusion that women were fostering. Then he will offer a solution.

Unlocking Meaning by Examining the Key Words

Now we will examine the meaning of the key words of this statement, "women", "silent", "speak", and "submissive".

Who were these "women" that Paul referred to in this passage? Knowing the answer to this will render the passage completely clear.

"Woman" Means "Wife"

Who were these "women" that Paul urged to keep silent?

The Greek has one word for "woman" but none for "wife." In order for us to know whether reference is made to all women or specifically to wives, we must examine the context. The mystery is solved when you read verse 34. Paul's recommendation that they ask their questions at home to their husbands makes it clear that the Greek word here is "wife" (married woman) not simply "woman." It cannot be a reference to "woman" because that would lead to the conclusion that the command to be silent was a universal principle for all members of the female gender, thus contradicting other Biblical passages. What it was that these women were talking about aloud we shall discover shortly, so we will not discuss that matter at this point.

"Silent" and "Speak"

If this second key word is to be taken literally, "silent" means to say nothing at all. Did Paul request absolute silence of the women he had just praised in verse 26 for their teaching, tongue-speaking, revelation, and interpretation? No way! Then what did he mean by the word "silent"? Permit me to offer three possible views of the meaning of this phrase and then offer reasons for the most logical one.

Returning to the passage in question (1 Corinthians 14:26-40), there are at least three views attempting to explain Paul's reason for the statement we read in vs. 35 above. Notice what Paul forbids the women to do. He says,

> "Let your women keep silent ... they are not permitted to speak."

I connect these two words because to understand the meaning of 'speak' is to know the true meaning of 'silent'. However, before I get to this exegesis, you need to know that there are at least other two prominent views that people espouse.

The other first view holds that Paul urged them to keep silent because they were spreading false doctrine (perhaps attempting to mix Gnostic views with apostolic teaching), and promoting that they could introduce disciples to "deeper knowledge". Hardly possible because, if true, Paul would have provided background information to substantiate this counsel.

The other second view insists that the Apostle's words were directed to the wives in the church but to a group who held this view: "it is shameful for women to speak in church." Unfortunately there is no evidence in the text or context to support this view—unless you count my Detractors.

These views are readily refuted by simply understanding the meaning of the Greek words. As I mentioned, once you know what "speak" means, the meaning of the word translated "silent" will become crystal clear.

Because verbal communication is so important, English has many ways to convey discourse, including scream, ramble, yell, whisper, and regale. But the most generic term is "to speak". Unfortunately, it is the easiest to misunderstand since it is the most ambiguous.

The Greek language has about a dozen words to convey, "to speak". However, only five of them have any relationship to preaching; and none of these are used by Paul in this verse. Rather, he chose the equivalent of "to speak," which in the Greek language is the word *laleo* (lay-LEH-oh). This word signified common ordinary conversation, i.e. people chatting. The word suggests that the people, upon entering the Assembly began to engage in friendly "chit-chat", which would escalate into a jumble of chatterbox conversations. And why not; they were simply exercising a freedom that the new life in Christ permitted. According to John Bristow (quoted earlier) "Paul was telling them that it is shameful for women to keep talking during the worship service."

Alan Redpath, a noted Bible scholar and former pastor of Moody Memorial Church in Chicago, observed that the word means "to talk, question, argue, profess, or chatter. It has nothing to do with prophecy or prayer; it is not public speaking as such."

Surely Dr. Redpath spoke correctly because in 1Cor. 11:1-16, Paul has already asserted the right of females to prophesy and pray in public.

Now that we understand the meaning of "to speak" let us connect it with the true meaning of the word "silent".

John Bristow says that "there is a word in Greek that means 'tie shut,' 'muzzle.' It is often used to describe a kind of forced silence, and perhaps it is best translated by our English idiom 'shut up.' "[57] That word, he said, is *phimoo (fim-OH-o),* which means "forcing someone to be silent."[58]

So, once again, exegesis resolves the question: Paul did not use *phimoo* when he commanded the women to be silent. Instead he used the word *sigao* which is a voluntary silence as opposed to a forced silence. Bristow said, "*Sigao (Sig-AH-o)* is the kind of silence asked for in the midst of disorder and clamor."[59]

While, at the outset of this chapter, we discussed the cultural setting of the Corinthian situation, let me add this comment since it will help you appreciate why the women may have engaged in so much chatter. In the first century church, patterned after the Jewish synagogue, the men sat together in one section, while the women, en masse, sat separately. As a result, these women who had tasted the first freedom in Christ to even speak in public, would react to another person bringing a prophetic message and yell out a question to their husbands seated across the room! For this reason, Paul then adds, "Let her ask her husband at home."

Once you grasp the picture of the scene inside that worship service, Paul's admonition makes sense: the place for discussing any question generated from the prophetic preaching is at home, not during the service since they interrupt the edification process and can disintegrate into dissension. It is this specific problem that Paul is warning about.

Now we can move on to analyze the third key word in the above verse, "submissive".

Submissive

The fourth key word is "submissive." On the question of submission, Greek scholars agree that the object of women's submission is not absolutely clear in the original language. The issue is resolved, however, when one realizes that the context necessitates that we consider the meaning of the word involved is dealing with ministry not marriage.

It is argued that the law does not teach submission of women to men. The creation account of Genesis chapters 2 and 3 speak of equality and partnership. We must assume that the wives were commanded to submit either to God, to the leadership of the Church, or to themselves (the spirit of the prophet is subject to the prophet), anyone of which is Biblical. What is clear, however, is that Paul is dealing with worship, not marriage. To say that all women ought to submit to all men in everything related to spiritual gifts is not Biblically sound.

Upon investigation, you discover that the Greek word chosen here by Paul is *hupotassomo,* expressing a voluntary attitude. Contrast this word with the other Greek word for slave-like obedience, *hupakouo* (hoop-ah-KOO-oh), used to signify the obedience required by slaves, hence not the word Paul selected for this passage.

In the phrase we are analyzing, we discover that the word *hupotassomo* was used for voluntary submission. To appreciate its meaning let us observe how it was used in connection with military service. When a group of soldiers was forming up as a unit to move out, a straggler would be told to join his group with this verb. Therefore, this word meant, "join up".

This word is also used in connection with the marriage relationship between a husband and wife. Ephesians 5:21 admonishes us to submit to one another in the fear of God. Notice how the meaning of this word brings clarity to what Paul meant by wifely submission. He intended to say that wives should "join up" and support their husbands, as unto the Lord. Paul's idea was for them to form a partnership that would provide mutual support, not slavish obedience. This will become even clearer when I point out that this verb, *hupotassomo* (in Eph. 5:21) occurs in the middle voice, signifying that it is an appeal by the Apostle to wives, i.e. a voluntary response. Think about it, submission of a wife means that she willingly, by her own volition, joins her support to her husband, and does not sound anything like the kind demanded by bullying husbands and over-bearing Detractors, does it?

Now, permit me to reinforce this view regarding women in the church. They are to voluntarily join their hearts, minds and wills to that of the prevailing leadership of the congregation. Does that strike you as a level of submission on par with a door mat?

For that misguided view of submission you will have to turn to those influenced by Socrates, and Aquinas.

With these four key words now clearly understood, there remains only one final piece of counsel from Paul. It is chilling.

Final Counsel: Ignore the Willfully Ignorant

As he concludes this counsel, Paul recognizes that his counsel may not be well received by some. He anticipates their objections and counters them with these words:

> What! Did the word of God originate with you, or are you the only ones it has reached? (1 Cor. 14:36)

Is Paul being satirical? Let's say he is being sardonic in an effort to head off the influence of Socrates that would lead them to oppose and ignore his counsel.

Evidently the congregation included those who felt that they were so knowledgeable in the teaching of the Spirit, that they could decide this issue without his apostolic help. So Paul addresses those inclined to reject his counsel:

> "If any one thinks that he is a prophet, or spiritual, he should acknowledge that what I am writing to you is a command of the Lord." (1 Cor. 14:37)

We should not be surprised at this tendency; it still exists. I know because often, when I was accosted by people claiming to be led of the Spirit, as I attempted to explain the true meaning of this passage, they would refuse to even consider the possibility that I might be right.

On the other hand, these words speak to me also; warning me not to ignore proper dress and demeanor or create empty words in the message I preach. To fall into these traps would be to lose the blessing of God and ruin the edification process for my own congregation and ministry gift, I would know it by the swift removal of blessing from my efforts.

Then Paul continues, with a final word to those in ministry leadership in 1 Cor. 14:38. We will examine the statement in English, and then provide you, dear reader, with a very precise translation from the Greek text.

First, this statement as it occurs in an English translation reads, "*If any one does not recognize this, he is not recognized*". Now permit me to make a most literal translation, "If any one be (willfully) ignorant, let him be ignored." Notice that Paul says, if someone ignores this warning, even after the true meaning has been presented to them, then do not pay attention to him; do not needlessly exalt him or her or even become embroiled in any debate with him/her about this subject. Paul's reason is chilling: If he will not listen to the authority of the Word, then do not give him a platform from which to speak; he deserves to be ignored by all people.

Last Words

To demonstrate that this entire discussion was about hindrances to edification, Paul offers these final words that return our thoughts to the central issue that the passage focused upon: "Let all things be done decently and in order."

3. Summary of Corinthian Insights

The nail that male supremacists are driving, based on their own interpretation of the passage, is that man is the head of woman.

When God created Adam and Eve, He gave both of them dominion, not over each other but "over the fish of the sea, over the birds of the air, and over the cattle, over all the earth and over every creeping thing."[60] After the fall, curses were put on the man, the woman, and the serpent.

To the woman He said: "...Your desire shall be for your husband, and he shall rule over you."[61]

The purpose of the death of Jesus Christ was to redeem the human race from the curse and to reinstate mankind. Before He went to the cross, Jesus called the disciples and gave them power "over unclean spirits, to cast them out, and to heal all kinds of sickness and all kinds of disease." [62]

Linda L. Belleville said, ". . . it is the church that possesses authority and not particular individuals (or positions, for that matter). It is to the church that Jesus gives the 'keys of the kingdom' (Matt. 16:19) and the authority to 'bind' and 'loose' (that is, enforce and waive) [Matt. 18:18]."[63] A careful study of the passage in question indicates that the text does not address male authority or female submission, neither is it about Divine nor hierarchical order, be it in the church or at the home.

ENDNOTES

53 Cunningham & Hamilton, 142.
54 Ibid.
55 Holy Bible,The New King James Version Red Letter Edition, *The Open Bible Large Print Expanded Edition*, (Nashville: Thomas Nelson Publishers, 1985). Introduction to the book of 1Corinthians.
56 Cunningham & Hamilton, 169.
57 Bristow, 62.
58 Ibid.
59 Ibid. , 63.
60 Gen. 1:26, (NKJV).
61 Gen. 3:16, (NKJV).
62 Mt 10:1.
63 Beck & Blomberg, 106.

Chapter 6

Ephesus Showdown

Clarifying Eph. 4 and 1 Tim. 2

1. Overview of Argument

By now, you know that whenever people challenge the legitimacy of my ministry, their arguments include four issues:

i) Women cannot assume leadership over men, since they are Divinely subordinate to male Headship
ii) The Bible restricts women from leadership in that they are mandated to keep silent to prevent Confusion
iii) The Bible insists that women keep silent in public worship to prevent Disorder
iv) Only men are called to the primary leadership positions of Apostle, Prophet, Evangelist, Pastor and Teacher.

The first two of these issues we addressed in the previous chapter. If one understands the exegetical arguments we supplied, and maintains an open mind, these issues are resolved; and cannot be used as a basis for ousting females from ministry leadership. We shall now focus on understanding the meaning of the last two issues which occur in two books written to Believers at Ephesus.

As the first two issues occurred in Pauline writing were addressed to a people living in a city dominated by a cult centered around the worship of a goddess Astarte, likewise Ephesus (to whom both final passages are addressed) also lay under the cultural grip of another (but similar) cult, centered on a goddess named Artemis.

To me, it makes sense that these issues would arise in churches whose membership had been regenerated from such pagan cultures. If these congregations had solely been made up of converted Jews perhaps the issues regarding women would not need to be addressed, since women in that culture were predisposed to never speak out. Only where the local cultures gave free rein to participate in civic and religious affairs on an equal basis with men, these issues were bound to arise.

In this chapter we will deal with two additional aspects of this issue: whether or not women in ministry leadership are usurping authority, or attempting to exercise gifts that were intended by God for men only.

To give you a brief look at the direction this discussion will take, the following "road map" will be helpful. Think of these topical divisions as milestones:

1. Introduction to Argument
2. Overview of the Ephesian worldview
3. Usurping Authority Issue Analysis (1 Tim. 2)
4. Clarification of the "Male Calling" Issue (Eph. 4)
5. Final Evidence of Women in Ministry Leadership
6. Summary of Argument

Our goal is to provide such a clear understanding of the true meaning of two of the four critical passages that they can never be used again by our Detractors. However, I must not only be right in my interpretation of these verses, but I must not violate sound hermeneutical analysis. To that end, we will begin with the first stage of analysis, examining the historical and cultural roots that shaped the worldview of the Believers in Ephesus regarding women in leadership. From this investigation we shall gain a perspective of the historical background of Paul's textual meaning.

2. Historical Setting for Ephesian Advice

When we analyzed the Corinthian passages we found that there was a cultural and philosophical connection to the issues of Headship and

Silence which stemmed from a special cultic religion that dominated the thinking and economy of Corinth.

Likewise, we are about to learn that a similar cult in Ephesus had spawned a worldview that resulted in misunderstanding and chaos within the Ephesian assembly regarding the roles of women, especially after a most unfortunate situation led to the removal of a female leader from ministry (which we shall address later on).

Was there ever a city more appropriate to discuss the issue of women in ministry leadership than Ephesus? The city was a world center for a very popular female centered cult that shaped the philosophical foundation on which the citizens built their view of the world and women.

Female religious leadership was as old as the city itself. Ephesus claimed that it had been founded by women warriors called Amazons whom they vowed were superior to male soldiers. These founders established the worship of the fertility goddess, Artemis. Her claim to fame was that, among other things, she could keep a woman safe during the dangers of childbirth; hence her name—"Artemis". It is a Greek word that means "to be safe".

The economy of Ephesus was built on the tourism business that served devotees traveling who would arrive from other parts of the world to participate in the religious activities.

All activities took place inside an enormous temple that dominated the city skyline. It was such an impressive structure that historians rate it as one of the seven wonders of the ancient world. At its front door, this Temple prominently displayed a towering statue of a nude, multi-breasted woman. Servicing the sexual needs as a religious experience generated an enormous income, as millions from all over the Mediterranean, poured into it annually.

The cult focused on creating devotees by offering sexual pleasures; and the kinkier the better. Yearly, the most desirable Virgin was paraded out to the devotees and one "lucky" gentleman spent the weekend of his life in her arms. To supply sufficient number of Temple prostitutes (so that every man and woman could "worship") women were recruited from locals. In fact, volunteering one's weekend to provide such practices was considered fashionable for even the well-to-do.

The cult was centered on the Female Goddess, Artemis. Permit me to share some of their more prominent tenets of this religion.

The Artemis cult claimed that Eve was created before Adam and received "special knowledge" when she ate the forbidden fruit. Paul addresses Eve and her true role in his First Epistle to Timothy; and no doubt, its relevance influenced his Epistle to the Ephesians.

The Artemis religion was popular because it incorporated sexual intercourse with a Temple prostitute into the worship experience using Mediator women who mixed sex with worship. The Greek word for Mediator is "Authenia" from the root word "Authenteo". We shall see this word used in two passages in this Epistle. The doctrine of female Mediators is countered in I Tim. 2:5 where Paul wrote that "...there is one Mediator between God and man, the Man, Christ Jesus."

The "Mediators" ("Authenia") of this religion claimed to be able to pass on "special knowledge" to men during sexual rites involving intercourse. A few verses later Paul wrote, "I do not permit a woman to teach or to "AUTHENTEIN" a man, but to be in silence." The connection between the religion and Paul's meaning here will become clear when we deal with this verse shortly.

The mystery religions and Gnostic beliefs shared many of these same beliefs. For this reason, Paul weaves into these epistles subtle remarks intended to rebut many of the tenets of the Artemis cult, and the worldview it spawned.

When you understand the attitude of Ephesian citizens toward women in cultic "ministry" you can appreciate why Paul felt it necessary to provide the true Believers of this city with careful instructions regarding the role of Christian women in public ministry.

Fortunately, the principles that he wrote about were not only relevant to the Ephesian believers who first heard the words, but also are relevant for all succeeding generations to the present day, including my incident at the Food Court when I was encountered by the two Christian men to whom I introduced you in chapter one. You will recall that their bone of contention was that I was "usurping" the man's "authority." To support their case, they used our first passage, 1 Tim. 2:12 (KJV), "But I suffer not a woman to teach, nor to usurp authority over the man, but to be in silence."

As I prepare to enter an exegetical surgical ward to determine the author's intended meaning, I am aware that I have entered upon a theological battlefield; therefore I will proceed with great caution since I have everything at stake. To appreciate this, consider my options based on the results of sound exegesis.

Option One: If it becomes impossible to exegetically reach a conclusion as to the clear meaning, then one must conclude that the Bible does not deserve to be the rule and authority of anyone's Christian faith.

Option Two: If the analysis proves to support the position of my Detractors, such as the one with which I was accosted in the Food Court, then I have no choice but to resign my pastorate. I confess that to do this would be the nearest thing to a death sentence after two decades of such whole hearted devotion.

Option Three: If the analysis renders a verdict that I do legitimately belong in ministry leadership; then my Detractors must obey Paul's admonition to "keep silent".

So as I begin the analysis of this passage, I do so with sense that I am entering a realm as dangerous as a mine field. Small wonder then, that I have, over the past decade, invested so much time and money for the educational training in exegeting the Scriptures in the language in which they were written, as my Doctoral degree bears evidence.

I have no other options. The solace I might receive by joining with those of the feminist movement who advocate for female pastors are not available to me, because, by rejecting the authority of Scripture, therefore any Biblical basis for women in leadership, I must reject the association due to my love for sound doctrine.

No, I choose to rest my case on the conclusions reached by exegetical analysis. I will live or die by the Bible's last word on the subject.

Yet I would be less than honest if I did not admit that I approach the task of surmounting this final textual mountain with hopefulness. This is because, after wrestling with the two previous issues, I know, without a doubt, that the pastorate I hold meets the approval of the Apostle Paul. However the issue before me is that I must be able to legitimately prove this to be true, again, in light of these two final issues. There can be no "string untied."

So, although nothing discovered so far would require me to tender my resignation from my vocational ministry position, nevertheless, I will approach the exegetical process with great care and respect. That being understood, I say, let us begin to thoroughly investigate this Biblical passage.

3. Authority Issue Revisits Silence Issue: 1 Tim. 2:8-10

These verses deal with how preaching and prayer leadership should be exercised rather than about who should lead them.

As we study them, we will discover that they provide counsel on the proper attitude for all genders as well as specific instruction for females in ministry leadership:

> "I desire then that in every place the men should pray, lifting holy hands without anger or quarreling; also that women should adorn themselves modestly and sensibly in seemly apparel, not with braided hair or gold or pearls or costly attire but by good deeds, as befits women who profess religion." (1 Tim 2:8-10).

Permit me to point out three important facts from this passage regarding leadership.

First, let me point out that some of this counsel is directed at both genders, since the reference to "men" is the Greek word for "mankind" not male gender. I view this as tacit acceptance of women in leadership by including them in this broad category of humans. Permit me to now deal with an analysis of that portion of Paul's admonition directed at both genders.

Gender Inclusive Counsel

Paul says that two conditions are required for all who lead in worship:

- 'Lifting up holy hands'
- Hearts free of anger or quarreling

These phrases are binding upon everyone, regardless of gender. I will now probe the meaning of each of these phrases.

Hands Clean Before God

Lifting one's hands was considered the normal posture in prayer, since the New Testament church incorporated the practice in Jewish synagogues.

Rabbinical leaders not only assumed the posture of standing with their arms lifted up, but led the congregation to assume the same posture.

However, Paul intended for the lifting of one's hands to be a metaphor. His point: ones external actions (clean hands) should mirror the condition of ones hearts, free of unconfessed sin. Nothing kills edifying worship like the removal of the Holy Spirit's participation which will occur if any ministry leader (regardless of gender) allows sin to prevent being filled, i.e., controlled by His Presence. That is the first condition for leadership: the leader must be in fellowship with God; no unconfessed sin. Next Paul speaks to a second condition.

Hearts Clean Before Men

The second condition: to provide spiritual leadership one's heart must be clean of any unresolved interpersonal issues. Notice the contrast. Whereas the first condition dealt with one's relationship with God, this second area of counsel deals with a leader's relationship with the people they serve, i.e., making sure that the leader harbors no ill feelings (bitterness, resentment, jealousy, anger, etc.) towards anyone being led. Only people not entangled in ongoing squabbles or harboring grudges are qualified to lead in prayer (and prophetic ministry).

So the first counsel of Paul is: make sure you are in fellowship with the Holy Spirit and free of any interpersonal relationship problems. It is directed at both genders. However, his next counsel is directed at female leaders.

The third qualification for ministry leadership is trickier to analyze. To guide your understanding, we will quote the English translation of the first part of the verse that makes up the passage we are analyzing, and then point out clues that unlock its meaning:

> "...also that women should adorn themselves modestly and sensibly in seemly apparel,"

Notice that two ideas are imbedded in this clause that will clarify its true interpretation.

Clue #1

Notice the word translated as "also" above? It is not the best translation because it implies that Paul is changing the subject, which is not true. The Greek word should be translated as, "in like manner." The accuracy matters since it confirms that he meant his remarks were directed toward females, thereby legitimizing their ministry. The accuracy also matters since it will establish that he did intend certain special conditions for female leadership.

Clue #2

Paul next describes the conditions by which females lead:

> "...women should adorn themselves modestly and sensibly in seemly apparel..."

Why were these aspects of demeanor and dress important? I will offer two reasons.

First, women must make sure that they violate no cultural mandates. Recall, from our discussion in Chapter 5, of the head covering issue? It was directly related to a female leader's compliance with local custom regarding dress code, which must not be violated.

Second, by obeying these rules of dress and demeanor, female leaders gain "leadership power" necessary to be able to effectively influence a congregation toward change. Modesty does for women leaders what "take charge/initiating" does for male leadership.

It is an extraordinary insight from Paul, and worth repeating: women gain leadership power by demonstrating modesty.

I know this is the correct interpretation, not only because the word meanings and syntactical analysis are supported by the laws of Hermeneutics; but also because this passage agrees exactly with what Paul says in First Corinthians 11 about women in the congregation. There, you will recall, he acknowledged that women must have their heads covered as a demonstration of their agreement with the principle of headship, i.e., by demonstrating modesty.

Is Paul, with these words, trying to regulate women's dress when he says that women should not have "braided hair or gold or pearls or costly attire..."? Yes and No:

"Yes", to the extent that such an extravagant display of wealth would project an immodest ostentation; and "No", since Paul's point is more about a metaphorical aspect of such accessories. His point: women's outward appearance must reflect a righteous inner spirit.

To appreciate Paul's point, imagine a woman attempting to lead a prayer wearing a provocative outfit. She would obviously not be trying to get God's attention; she may be seeking to garner the attention of the men in attendance. Her choice of wardrobe and accessories would reveal her heart. Such modesty would convey that she is not trying to draw attention to herself but showcase a godly attitude.

Therefore, as a result of her righteous demeanor and appearance, she provides no blockage of the Holy Spirit's free release of His power to accompany her words, resulting in changed lives and answered prayers.

What a contrast to the sexually provocative, lewd leadership of the Artemis cult of which these people were most familiar. Such wise insights from Paul!

4. Silence Issue and Edifying Calm: 1 Tim 2:11-14

Now we come to the central issue –the conditions that make it possible for a woman to exercise spiritual leadership to produce edifying worship:

> "Let a woman learn in silence with all submissiveness. I permit no woman to teach or to have authority over men; she is to keep silent; for Adam was formed first then Eve; and Adam was not deceived, but the woman was deceived and became a transgressor." (1 Tim. 2:11-14).

To understand the meaning of this text will require you knowing what is meant by three key phrases:

- "have authority over"
- "keep silent"
- "Eve" reference

A clear understanding of these phrases will unlock the true interpretation of the passage.

"Have Authority Over"

To achieve an edifying ministry, a female leader must guard against using the wrong kind of power in the exercise of her spiritual gift. Ironically, the Greek word for "authority" ("authentein") comes from the same word that describes the cult, i.e., "Artemis". It means, "to domineer, to usurp authority, to take what is not rightfully yours." This idea has several important connections to women in ministry leadership.

First, it will destroy her access to true power, via the use of modesty. Modesty works because it relies on the Holy Spirit; in usurping authority the woman is declaring that she will use masculine ways to attempt to gain power to change lives—and that cannot work.

Second, it destroys the purpose for her leadership, i.e., edifying worship since in using the wrong type of "power" she creates disorder, making it impossible for the congregation to function in peaceable quietness, as we shall discover momentarily.

Third, by asserting her will in an autocratic manner, as if she is the final authority in all matters of doctrine, she destroys any hope for her message to produce edification. The reason is simple: it will imply that her interpretation is true because she says so, thereby removing the partnership of the Holy Spirit. The ultimate basis for any Biblical interpretation must reside in the Word itself, since it originated in God's mind, was revealed by the Holy Spirit, and is only possible to understand by His illumination.

My Detractors, because they used this word wrongly, would be surprised to learn that I whole-heartedly agree with Paul's counsel regarding this Greek word, "authentein".

I have built my pulpit leadership by interpreting the Word of God according to the rules of sound Hermeneutics that produce clarity. Any interpretation I present as a sermon is not true because I say so, but because the rules of sound Hermeneutics have determined it to be correct. The power to change lives is the result of three factors: integrity, clarity, and relevance. By rightly dividing the Biblical passage I am preaching or teaching, I gain clarity and relevance. By the use of modesty, I demonstrate integrity.

Should I resort to asserting that I am the last word in doctrinal decisions and "pushing my weight around," because of my position of authority, then the results would never edify or produce change.

This key word deals with the first condition for effective female leadership. Now we will consider the second key word that unlocks the meaning of this passage.

"Keep Silent"

Now we come to the second condition for edifying worship from women pastors: leadership that does not generate controversy but rather, promotes "peaceableness", which involves understanding the meaning of the phrase, "keep silent".

At first blush, it seems we are returning to the discussion we had regarding the phrase "keep silent" in the 1 Cor. 14:26-40 passage we analyzed in the previous chapter. However, an analysis of the Greek word shows that here, Paul uses a completely different word from "laleo" meaning "chit-chat". Here the word translated as "keep silent" is an entirely different word in the Greek language, the word, hesychia ("hes" "sick" "i" "ah"), translated as "silence". Its meaning: a state of mind characterized by an attitude of peaceable quietness. It suggests a state of sustained tranquility, free of turmoil and political uproar.

The basis for the silence is the speaker has become calm resulting in the cessation of speech, action, or conflict.[64] Herodotus used the word to describe a quiet disposition.

To help you, dear reader, to gain a deeper understanding of this word's intended meaning, let me describe how Paul uses the word in 1Timothy 2:2 and in 2 Thessalonians 3:12. They provide additional insight to help us understand the true meaning of this word.

In 1 Tim.2:2 the word *authentein* occurs in this sentence: "We are to pray for kings and all who are in high positions, that we may lead a quiet and <u>peaceable</u> life." However, unlike the English translation "silent" in 1Tim. 2:11-14, it is translated in 1Tim. 2:2 as "peaceable".

If I were now in the Food Court with my Detractors I would point out that the true meaning of the word has to do with all leaders (including female) striving to live a life undisturbed by conflict and hassle, i.e., a "peaceable" life.

2 Thessalonians 3:12

As a background to this passage, understand that Paul has just concluded describing certain persons as "busybodies". In 2 Thess. 3:12, he adds (regarding these busybodies): "Now such persons (busybodies) we command and exhort in the Lord Jesus Christ to do their work in quietness." Here *authentein* is translated as "quietness" to make the point that people should go about their work in a peaceable manner, i.e. not willfully attempting to draw public attention to themselves. The context makes it clear that Paul did not mean that they should remain continually silent.

So what light does these two uses of our word shed on its meaning in our passage? We discover that Paul means to caution females involved in ministry leadership to maintain an attitude that is reasonable, patient, and willing to listen to others, and in the course of exercising their leadership gifts, conduct themselves modestly in order to maintain the unity of the Body in the bond of peace. When one understands the culture in which the Ephesian church functioned, it is clear why Paul felt compelled to address this issue of female "silence" in relation to edification in worship.

We are analyzing three key words in the above passage that unlock its true interpretation.

We will now deal with the third, which is not specifically stated but implied in the statement, "...for Adam was formed first then Eve; and Adam was not deceived, but the woman was deceived and became a transgressor." (1Tim. 2:14).

What does this have to do with edifying worship by female leaders? Much!

Implications of Eve's Actions

Having established the conditions by which a woman ministers the Word (in peaceable- ness and asserting not her own will but God's), Paul now returns to the discussion begun earlier in this chapter, using Eve's actions to make a new point.

First, he refutes the notion espoused by the Artemis cult regarding Eve being created before Adam (therefore, they insisted, women leaders were meant to be superior to men, thereby giving women the "authority" over men). His words are a fatal blow, attempting to rid the congregation of even the hint of this evil philosophy.

His second reason is to use Eve's handling of the Temptation as a metaphor to explain areas in which each sex is vulnerable to leadership pitfalls.

In the Genesis narrative, Adam was first created and given the task, as an initiator, of naming all the animals. To fulfill his task, Adam had to gain a thorough understanding of the natural world by investigating all animals (and plants). On the basis of what he learned he gave them names describing important facts gleaned that all species existed as gender pairs, except his own. As a result, his first remark as he meets Eve for the first time reveals something important about himself, "At last! Finally, I have found that which completes me, corresponds to me, is equal to me, and is sent to help me fulfill the task which God has given me to do."

Next, the Genitive narrative shows that they approach their assigned tasks differently, based on their genders. Paul will use this gender distinctiveness as a metaphor to show that in regard to the task of leadership, there is a difference in their approach. We discussed this in the previous chapter: men derive power by initiating, i.e., starting things; they are entrepreneurs. This is why Adam was sent first into the world. This is not to say that women cannot initiate things for indeed they do.

On the other hand, women generally lead by taking that which has been initiated and nurturing it into completion. They are managers, care-givers. They achieve change by consoling and comforting something toward wholeness.

But, then Paul uses this truth as a metaphor. His point: their distinctiveness also makes them vulnerable to failing in different ways.

He then speaks to female leaders: Eve's submission to Satan's lie was due, says Paul, to her natural tendency (as a female) to comfort and complete. As a result, she forgot that the first responsibility was to obey the Word of God not to eat the fruit of the Tree of the Knowledge of Good and Evil.

Likewise, the female pulpiteer can fall into the same gender trap: she must not bring comfort and wholeness that fails to properly stress the responsibility of the "pew" to obey the clear mandate of the Biblical text she is proclaiming.

What caused Eve to sin? She felt she was doing a right thing; something, in fact, that could benefit her husband and herself. Paul's point is that her instinct for nurturing and care-giving rendered her vulnerable to Satan's attack. He wants to show that this distinctive of female leadership must be handled with watchfulness that it will not be used in a bad way.

It is the glory of woman that she is more responsive than man to what is around her. That is what makes life beautiful. How dull and cold and barbarous life would be if all we had was the contribution of men! Women add that quality of tenderness, softness, empathy, sympathy and comfort to the world. They add something that no man can give.

Yet think of the progress in the world and the Kingdom that has resulted from the leadership of men who study a problem or inhumane condition for mankind or creature comforts, and pro-actively initiate a solution to the problem and bring about progress.

To appreciate the differences between the sexes in leadership, permit me to use this illustration: consider the relationship between a knife and fork. They do not perform the same functions, yet we use them at the same time while we are eating to accomplish a common goal even though we employ them in different ways. Likewise, when it comes to the goal of preaching and teaching the Word, a male will handle the responsibility differently than a woman, even though the goal is the same. That is what Paul is driving at. Incidentally, psychologists and sociologists are beginning to recognize these same differences between men and women exercising leadership.

Now that we know that this passage does not disqualify women from leadership but only lays down certain ground rules based on gender uniqueness, we can now harvest the remaining insights regarding women in leadership found in verses 15 and 16:

> "Yet woman will be saved through bearing children, if she continues in faith and love and holiness, with modesty." (1 Tim 2:15)

Again, Paul is using the word "saved" and the phrase, "bearing children" metaphorically to show that her commitment to obey his counsel concerning how to lead (as a woman) will result in blessed results which validate the legitimacy of her leadership.

"Saved"

In the Hebrew culture, the people were farmers, therefore, their financial welfare and future was tied to maintaining the tract of land allotted to their Tribe by Joshua. Unfortunately, if they had no children to inherit the land, it was redistributed by Tribal leaders to others. That prospect made barrenness heartbreaking. This fact Paul uses as a metaphor. His point: As the woman fulfilled her "wifely" calling by childbearing, so a woman fulfills her calling to preach the Gospel by bearing fruit. This becomes clear when you understand this unique Greek word translated as "saved".

In the Bible there are two words for "saved"; one deals with eternal salvation, while the other one means "to find fulfillment," i.e., "to achieve meaning, and significance." Again, we shall observe how this word is used elsewhere to get a clear understanding of its meaning.

In1Tim. 4:16 we discover this same word translated as "saved":

> "Take heed to yourself and to your teaching; hold to that, for by so doing you will **save** (the same word as in 1 Tim. 2:15) both yourself and your hearers."

Since Timothy was already redeemed, this word must deal with the meaning described above, meaning "to be fulfilled," i.e., "to find significance." Plug this meaning into the word 'saved' and the passage suddenly becomes clear.

Paul is saying to women, "Your fulfillment in the role God has given you as authoritative teachers in a church will come as a result of the correct handling of your teaching gifts and calling, as well as the way you comport yourself with modesty; and remain on guard as to potential areas of vulnerability unique to your gender. Fulfill these conditions and you will find meaning and significance." The expression, "bearing (spiritual) children", is a metaphor for fruitfulness related to people being saved and the worship being marked as "edifying". Also, such "children" confirm the legitimacy of her calling as a woman to ministry leadership.

To appreciate the truth of this interpretation of the metaphorical aspect of this verse, think of the real fact on which it is based—physical motherhood. As a mother of earthly children finds her fulfillment in pouring herself and her values into her children in order that they grow to healthy productive adulthood because of her influence, so the woman in ministry leadership will find fulfillment when her ministry produces lives that grow to maturity in faith. That is what the apostle is talking about.

In summary, what a wealth of insights from this passage: women were given access to the role of ministry leadership by Paul, yet they must approach the task with certain provisos in relation to the goal of their task (worship that edifies). They must not ignore the correct source of their authority in modesty. As a result, they must not seek to assert their will in a manner inappropriate to their gender, thereby wrecking any hope for producing unity and tranquility in the Body. Also, they must remain sensitive to the fact that their special approach to leadership can produce disastrous results if they fail to stay focused on the primary responsibility of their calling, as Eve did. Finally, if they maintain this mindfulness, there is a promise of having their ministry validated by genuine fruitfulness.

Now we turn to the fourth and final Biblical passage that my Detractors have leveled at me: Ephesians 4:11, and 12, they insist, prove that I must, in good conscience, resign my pastoral calling since the Bible proves that only men were given the primary leadership gifts (apostleship, evangelism, prophetic, pastoral, and teaching ministries). Are they right?

5. Are Leadership Gifts Reserved for Men Only?

Ephesians 4:11, 12

As I have presented the Gospel to thousands of people over the years, I have learned that I cannot convince anyone of its truth who willfully refuses to accept the truth, including Detractors insisting that the Bible can be used to support any argument.

I wonder if they realized how dangerous such a view is, since, if this assertion was true, we could not trust any promise of the Bible. Are these people aware that the only valid record of the One who died for our sins is in this Book?

The Scriptures are the result of supernatural revelation; yet, the product is governed by the vocabulary and syntax of the language in which it was written. Therefore, by use of the tools of exegesis in accord with the laws of Hermeneutics, the meaning of any passage can be determined—beyond reasonable doubt. In one sense, this is why I felt it worth the time and finances to learn this process, even though I had to study Hebrew and Greek. However, the Masters and Doctorate that I earned are not nearly as valuable to me as knowing that I can know, with certainty, the meaning of any passage since people's eternal destinies hang in the balance. I could not bear to attempt to guide people's lives if there were no true basis for hope. Neither would I want to serve as a pastor if the Word did not support the legitimacy of my calling.

Also, the promises relevant to salvation are no more true than the verses that authorize my ministry as a woman. Unfortunately, my Detractors seem adept at agreeing with my interpretation regarding the plan of salvation, but feel confident that I am completely misguided when I apply the same Hermeneutical rules to determining the legitimacy of women in leadership. Could it be that Socrates has cast his philosophic shadow over their minds?

We have already faced the arguments shaped by Socratic thinking over the first three Biblical passages that deal with women in ministry. We now stand before the final verses that deal with the source of those gifts essential to calling. The question my Detractors raise is one that I accept, and will now answer: "Did not Paul say that the gifts of leadership (Apostleship, Pastor, etc.) were given to men?" This question brings me to the threshold of the fourth passage that has been leveled at me, Ephesians 4:11, and 12.

I love this beautiful Epistle. It was the result of an extraordinary heavenly vision in which Paul was taken into the Presence of God and shown the Divine Plan of Salvation, and the role of each person of the Trinity in accomplishing it as well as the future of the world, the church, and the struggle with Satan. As a result of what he was shown, Paul wrote three Letters that touch on it: Philemon, Colossians, and our Epistle, Ephesians.

To confirm my interpretation, simply study the first twelve verses of chapter one and you will see the truth of my assessment.

His experience also influenced the shape of the Epistle. The first part deals with our position in Christ. Then section two (Chapter one through three) speaks to this question: if this is our position in the living God, then how should we then live? Chapter four picks up the discussion begun in chapter three regarding the living church. He then, in verses eleven and twelve, declares that the strength of the church in its path from new birth at the Upper Room until the end of Armageddon will be through each person receiving spiritual gifts that make their participation in building the Kingdom indispensable to their local congregations and His purpose.

Of these gifts, those reserved for strategic leadership are mentioned at the outset. Theologians like to distinguish these five gifts from the many others by saying these gifts are so imbued within the individual who receives them that they become the center of his life, vocationally. As a result, all other gifts are just gifts, and these are considered "callings", since they result in life-consuming ministry, which, in our culture often leads to vocational ministry assignments.

When you realize how strategic they were in the first years of the formation of the church you, at once, realize that they are very important. Today, the most prominent of them, the Pastor, or as some conclude, the Pastor-Teacher, accounts for most of those in vocational ministry.

The final section, dealing with how the true believer handles the reality of evil is one not relevant to our discussion; hence, we only mention it here so you can see the complete breakdown of the Epistle's message.

With this sweeping overview I return to the issue before me. My Detractors argue that the point of the verse in Eph. 4:8 is that these gifts were given to ***men*** (italics and emphasis mine). Perhaps, as I combine the appropriate Biblical text, you will see the gist of their argument:

> "Wherefore he saith, When he ascended up on high, he led captivity captive, and gave gifts unto **men**...some apostles; and some, prophets; and some, evangelists; and some, pastors and teachers;" (Eph. 4:8, 11KJV, emphasis mine)

Having rested their case on the English translation they feel confident in asserting that this is an "open and shut" case. The gifts could not have been given to a woman since she is of the wrong gender. So the question they leveled at me like a loaded gun was, "Then you (a female) have no business assuming a role that demands a gift you could not possess since it was intended for males only?"

My response to such an accusation is simple: If that is what the author intended the verse to say you would be correct and I would have to resign my pastorate. But does the Greek support the translation? (The question seems logical to me since it was penned by Paul in that language). The question mine begs is this: Is it hermeneutically sound to build a theological position on a translated word (English), or the source word of that translation (Greek)? Clearly, to locate a word that will enable one to find enough 'legitimacy' to impose a pre-conceived theological idea on a text is called eisegesis, a major violation of sound Biblical analysis.

So, then, toward clarity on this issue, what is the word used in the original text, since that will determine the proper English equivalent for a proper translation? In other words, what is the proper meaning of the Greek word translated as "men"?

Koine Greek has two words that can be used for our English word "*man*". The first is ανερ which we will transliterate as "aner".[65] The second Greek word is **ανθρωποσ**, which we shall transliterate as 'anthropos'. So what is the difference in meaning between these two Greek words?

The Greek word, *aner,* is used only of the male gender, never used of the female gender.[66]

In contrast, the Greek word *anthropos* is used generally of "a human being", including both male and female genders. In other words, the word *anthropos* is "gender-inclusive", i.e., referring to both men and women. One word best encompasses this meaning of the word in English: "humankind". I focus on this word because this is the Greek word used in Eph. 4:8.

Therefore, there can be no doubt about it, the "men" receiving these special leadership gifts were all members of one race, humanity that includes both genders. One might translate the word *anthropos* as "man the human" (i.e. humankind) or man as a "person" (i.e. man as either male or female gender). That is the word for man that occurs in the above passage, "and He gave gifts to ***men***". For the argument of my Detractors to be valid, the Greek word would have to be *aner*, the Greek word for "men", as meaning of the male gender. Since that word does not exist there, their argument is rendered completely wrong.

Based on the laws of Hermeneutics, only one legitimate conclusion is permitted: Ephesians 4:8 could not be used to exclude born again members of the female gender. Second, the Greek word used in Ephesians 4:8, is the word *anthropos*, NOT *aner*.

Therefore, the proper English translation should be,

> "He . . . gave gifts to the ***species called human beings...***"
> "... to be apostles, prophets, evangelists, pastors and teachers."

Can there be any doubt that God intended the female gender to be included among the gifted people given to lead the church? Sound exegesis dictates the answer to be a resounding "no!"

Conclusion

Currently, a number of church organizations and denominations around the world give women freedom to lead in areas where they are most gifted. I wonder, as I observe this phenomenon, why these organizations release their women into ministry? Is it frustration, on the part of the male fraternity, of not being able to do the work alone? In other words are they prompted by the magnitude of the task that necessitates more personnel?

Or could it be that these people have investigated the proper interpretation of these verses and concluded that women belong in ministry leadership?

In the course of waging this battle for the right of women to hold vocational positions of leadership, we have dealt at length with so many aspects of this argument. However, we must now step back from the close inspection of the Biblical meaning, to summarize the main tenets of our case, and look more at the issues in a context apart from the exegesis.

But before we do, we will face one last dark question: what about women in leadership that abuse their callings? There are, unfortunately many (as are there many men who do the same). So we will see how Paul dealt with a woman who moved from being a blessing to the kingdom to a complete menace. The study of Hymenaeus confirms the point of my argument (she was legitimately called to ministry) and at the same time bears testimony that one must guard the gifts one has been given to make sure they are used for the Savior and not for Satan. It will also prepare us to consider the next Section—where we will see the many women that God used from the Old Testament to the modern era in leadership.

6. A Female Minister Gone Bad

Paul mentions this woman twice in his letters to the Ephesians via Timothy (I Tim. 1:20 and 2 Tim. 2:17.) She, with her male accomplices, Alexander and Philetus, were ousted from the Ephesian congregation after having occupied a prominent place of leadership.

Her name may provide a clue to her personality. Her name means "Wedding Song", after the name of Hymen, the Greek god of marriage. Can you sense this could only have occurred in a town steeped in the culture of pagan Artemis worship? [67]

Her Career

In both references to her, it is important to note that she was considered a leader in the Ephesian congregation. Paul concedes that she was a true believer in Christ, therefore, urges Timothy to consider the long term consequence of her returning to the fellowship in Ephesus (1 Tim. 1:20). She must have been an effective preacher because her sermons had "overthrown the faith of some" (2 Tim. 2:18).

Her Crime

Unfortunately, she began to use her prophetic gift to promote her own interpretation. In prideful ignorance, her ideas moved to error worthy of being called blasphemous. She then used her prophetic ministry to blaspheme the teaching of the Lord, thereby serving Satan to shipwreck the faith of many by teaching this false doctrine: "the resurrection is past already." She used her gift to argue that the Believers should not look forward to any bodily resurrection at all nor the awakening of the soul from sin's existence since the resurrection had already taken place. In this she promoted an idea which John 5:28 confirms as heretical.

Historians speculate that her heretical ideas sprang from being influenced by Gnosticism. Their contempt for the physical body led them to deny the resurrection in its literal sense; and all that Christ had taught on the subject was explained only, in an allegorical sense, of the resurrection of the soul from sin.

As a result, she promoted the idea that the resurrection must be spiritualized to be understood, since (according to them), a physical resurrection violated the Gnostic idea that anything of material substance was inherently evil, therefore, if man is to rise from the dead he must rid himself of a human body since it was sinful. She then argued that since the Christians still had their bodies, the resurrection must have already taken place.

Paul, in 1 Cor. 15, shreds this false thinking as dangerous as gangrene, since if the literal resurrection of Christ is denied, Christian believers are yet in their sins, and the Christian religion is false.

Small wonder then that Paul urged Timothy to deliver the three apostates into the hands of Satan that they might be taught not to blaspheme. The important thing to note is that the purpose for this sentence was distinctly remedial. Paul desires that they come, via the discipline of Satan, to repentance and be returned to the fellowship at Ephesus.

Surely, their wickedness was a fulfillment of Paul's prophecy given to the Ephesian Elders years earlier, at the occasion of his farewell to them when he said, "I know that after my departing grievous wolves shall enter in among you, not sparing the flock; and from among your own selves shall men arise, speaking perverse things, to draw away the disciples after them" (Acts 20:29). Surely it was a reference to the gangrenous-like teaching of Hymenaeus and her male culprits.

So why bring up this example of Hymenaeus? How does her story illustrate our contention that the Apostle Paul intended for females to be in ministry leadership?

Hymenaeus could never have wielded such influence if she had not first been given the position of a female who spoke to the entire congregation. Her gifts had been recognized and her appointment to spiritual office had followed suit. It is most unfortunate that she exploited her gifts for evil. Yet, so did her male leader companions.

My only point was that she illustrates that women, even those who turned from using their gifts to glorify the Lord and apostatized nevertheless illustrate the reality: the Apostle Paul, and his disciple, Timothy, were convinced that women belonged in leadership.

Conclusion

Now that we have completed the exegetical analysis of each Biblical passage my Detractors use to prove that women do not belong in leadership, we need to step back and look at the four issues these passages represent. This we will do in the following chapter, designed to summarize our argument by including all the points we have confirmed as well as looking at some wider implications of these issues.

ENDNOTES

64 Theological Dictionary of the New Testament, Zondervan.
65 W.E. Vine, Merril F. Unger, & William White, Jr., *Vine's Complete Expository Dictionary Of Old and New Testament Words.*
66 Ibid.
67 Rutherfurd, John. "Hymenaeus," *International Standard Bible Encyclopedia.* Edited by James Orr. Volume 2 page 238)

Chapter 7

Revisiting Part Two

In the USA, hunting dogs are highly prized by sportsman. As a result, they command large prices.

The story is told of a sportsman who invited a potential customer to observe an expensive dog's skills tracking rabbits. After repeated failed attempts to catch a rabbit, the dog dropped at his owner's feet, exhausted and empty handed.

"Well", remarked the potential customer, " I thought you said he always gets his rabbit? What happened?"

"Hmm", replied the owner, " I guess it proves this fact: nothing running for its supper can catch something running for its life."

The information presented in Part Two grew out of the argumentative "give and take" I repeatedly faced defending myself against my Detractors. As they would raise an issue, I would turn to the Bible for answers to refute their charge. In time, I understood their thinking, and became increasingly adept at refuting their arguments.

Later, as I reflected on my capability I suddenly knew its motive. They were defending their own *status quo,* while I was defending my reason for being. In every debate I faced the possibility that I might hear an argument that proved them right. I would have to resign my pastorate, a chilling thought.

Finally, I began to realize that after so many encounters and subsequent reflections, I had built, with the Lord's help, a reasoned defense of why women belong in ministry leadership. As I shared these truths with others, the Lord used them to urge me to reduce all that I had learned on this subject to writing which you are reading.

Part Two has been a battle waged over the cultural roots of this issue and the correct interpretation of those passages that uniquely speak to its four primary facets. We weighed into the debate concerning each of the four relevant Biblical passages. Upon reflection it occurred to me that before we change the direction of our discussion of this issue that we should stop, step back, and take a broader view of the issues to which each passage speaks. It is appropriate that you see our case in a succinct manner. To that end we will present a summary of the salient arguments realized by proper exegesis. But I also want to just talk with you; to share thoughts regarding the four issues at the center of this controversy.

I do so because I feel it important to separate the issues from the textual analysis, once the text has validated Paul's intended meaning. That is why I spent the ink in an introductory chapter for Part Two to explain the only scientific process for knowing the meaning of Paul's words. Those laws rescued me from the evil practice of eisegesis. They also were my only hope for making a case that at the end of the day will stand up to complete scrutiny by those who genuinely want to know what the Bible says concerning these passages.

Still, I leave it to you, dear reader, to make the final judgment as to the validity of my argument. However, this chapter will provide you a compact presentation of all that has been said throughout the last three chapters. You will recognize it as a summary. I view it as a victory lap similar to that which the winner of an automobile race enjoys.

Arguments Supporting Women in Ministry Leadership

In conformance to sound exegesis we first looked at the historical roots of this issue. Our quest was to trace the cultural roots of this issue and its impact on the Corinthian and Ephesian congregations to which these four Biblical passages were addressed.

We discovered the philosophical "headwaters" of the "male only" ministry advocates. We then traced its evolution from Socrates to the modern era. Permit me to revisit the path this terrible idea has taken to wrap its tentacles around so much of the denominations and church leaders.

Cultural Roots of the Issue

Our first shocking discovery was that although the detractor view holds sway over many theologians since Augustine, this view was never based on Biblical reasoning. How amazing when you think I was accosted by those who believed their cause was Biblically based!

I am convinced none of the opposition realizes that their arguments stem from a Greek philosopher who built the male-only leadership philosophy espousing the superiority of men over women in every area except housework based on defending his own homosexuality. What Socrates initiated, Plato expanded, and his disciple, Aristotle perfected in the man who would infect western civilization with its ideas.

Aristotle was the man chosen by a king to tutor his son, Alexander, who grew up to become an extraordinary warrior and conquered the known world. The ideas he had learned from Aristotle he infected into every culture; the process was called "Hellenizing them", i.e., converting them to embrace the Greek worldview and values.

After the conclusion of the second Captivity, it wove its venom into even the Jewish culture. Every Pharisee at the time of Jesus began each day thanking God that he was not a woman.

Ironically, Jesus and Paul both rejected this thinking regarding women in leadership. Both embraced the concept that women belonged in ministry leadership and, in fact, trusted them with important ministerial responsibilities.

Unfortunately, only a few decades after Paul went to heaven, the male leaders of the New Testament, known as the Church Fathers reverted to Socratic thinking and reduced the role of women to pleasure and servitude. As far as ministry was concerned, they were unanimous: no females need apply.

How did men like Tertullian, Augustine and Ambrose, with such excellent reputations for theological soundness, lose their way so tragically on this issue? After much reflection, I feel that it happened because of four reasons.

First, the role of women within a few generations of Paul's time had been reduced to that specified by the Pharisees. Under their dictatorial "thumbs" there was no room for debate; Socratic thinking, couched as "godly interpretation of the Torah" carried the day with zero tolerance for female participation in spiritual debate.

Second, it never occurred to church leaders that their views concerning this issue stemmed from such a godless and non-Biblical source such as homosexual based philosophy. They embraced Socrates' disciple, Plato, because he had written so cogently to express one of the most important theological ideas—the ontological argument for the existence of God. So, in their esteem for him, they failed to question his views concerning women in leadership.

Third, although they knew the Scriptures, they were not drawn to build their faith from *Scriptura sola* argument until the Reformation writers, like Luther and Calvin, developed the science of using the Bible to explain its words, i.e., development of the only hermeneutical law for those whose faith is Biblically based.

Finally, these Church Fathers ignored something that the Apostle Paul insisted upon: the roles of men and women are always assigned by the prevailing culture. Church history leaders preferred to embrace the "maxim" that in the Biblical account of Adam and Eve there lay the roots of every cultural issue relevant to Christians. Unfortunately, they were only half right in this assumption. They also assumed that Paul's counsel concerning the relationship of men and women in the marriage relationship was mirrored in the relationship of women to men in ministry leadership. As we have seen, this was not the case.

Nevertheless, these godly men, devoted to the Lord and to His Word, absolutely missed the Bible's assertion that women belong in ministry leadership. Unfortunately, their stature in church history ensured that their error would be embraced *en toto* even into the present hour.

Modern Female Clergy and Feminism

Tucker & Liefeld said that a factor that has contributed to this problem in the modern era is that its major advocates have been females with a feminist impulse.[68] The assessment of these two writers: "Both feminists and traditionalists have lent their support to this view" but, "to the contrary" what we have found is "that most (non-feminist) women seemed very hesitant to challenge the 'rightful' leadership of men."[69]

Speaking about women in ministry, Tucker & Liefeld said, "Rarely have they manifested purely feminist qualities; rather, they are cautious of seeking a place of prominence in the church. When they do strive for positions in ministry, their motivation appears to be to serve more effectively."[70]

I understand this problem so well. I have had to continually clarify that my position was based on Biblical argument, and not on any political alignment with this movement that I find, in large part, embraces much that is contrary to Scripture.

In the past few decades we have witnessed the upsurge of female ecclesiastical leadership, particularly in the modernistic traditional Protestant denominations. Sadly, behind their advocacy is an undercurrent of sexual energy—often spawned by those females who have chosen a clerical profession for political purposes, or in an effort to promote the homosexual lifestyle.

Some within this movement have used the platform gained by ministry leadership to espouse views both bizarre and blasphemous. For example, consider their insistence that the Trinity should be re-examined from a non (male) chauvinistic position and the titles for "God the Father" be changed to "God the Mother"; that of Christ, to "Christa" a feminist caricature of the Jesus of the Bible. They also prefer to think of the Holy Spirit as "the Womb of God". They promote this with blasphemous bumper-stickers that invite people to "Trust in God, She loves you". Can you see why I have solidly distanced myself from this movement?

I reject every shred of this rhetoric, and flatly deny every tenet of such false doctrine. I say this to make sure that the issue remains focused on dealing with the true issues of this argument.

If I did not know that God has called me to this ministry, validated by equipping me with the gifts to lead a congregation, I would have no interest in pursuing the clergy vocation. In fact, as I reject the feminist view of women in ministry, I also reject the idea of ministry as a good paying job for a woman (or a man for that matter).

Seminaries are populated by many women who are in pursuit of a professional career that generates a handsome income. That idea never occurred to me. My early ministry was carried out as a non-paid lay preacher. It was there that I first incurred the Detractors. If my goal had been only to find myself a source of a comfortable income, the onslaught of these people, confronting me at every turn, would surely have dissuaded me.

In making these statements I realize that I am at once alienating many women who might find, in my struggle, a kindred spirit. However, in the long run all women will be well served by someone establishing a Biblical based justification for females in leadership, which is my goal.

Cultural Issues: Socrates to Corinth and Ephesus

No need to revisit, in detail, information already covered in the previous chapters. Suffice the review here to mention that these churches, in cities dominated by sexual cults under female control, made them perfect for Paul to speak to our issue. It makes sense that a philosophy concerning the role of women in society based on sex would produce such perverted fruit as prostitution in the name of religion. Also, I find it fascinating that Paul, with his Jewish heritage, would speak so clearly; to me it indicates he was obeying the Lord to get His will on paper in these Epistles, rather than falling back to his own Pharisaical worldview.

Also, I am convinced that my Detractors had no clue as to the true roots of the views they espoused. After all, there is a "who's who" of religious leaders, Jewish and Christian, between their convictions and the true Socratic roots. Yet, although they were acting out of misguided convictions, nevertheless, they were dead wrong, and willing to draw blood in a battle of wits with me. Should I have caved in to their urging and ceased my ministry they would have reported this with rejoicing that the Word of God had prevailed. Sadly, their wrong-headedness raises this question: if they were so misguided as to the cultural basis for their argument, how far afield were their Biblical reasons? It is something to consider as we now proceed to summarize the Biblical analysis for each passage that speaks to the issue of women in ministry leadership.

Summary of Biblical Arguments Supporting My Position

As we launch this review, let us understand the four components of this issue:

- The matter of a woman usurping the authority of male leadership
- The necessity for covering
- The necessity of women remaining silent in church
- Spiritual gifts appropriate for leadership are only divinely available for males

Notice that I have rearranged the order from that in which they were discussed in the previous chapters. The idea behind the change was to look at them in a fresh way, even though I intend to include summaries of the arguments made previously.

Issue: Usurping Authority

You will also recall my encounter with the two Christian men at the food court. Their bone of contention was that I was "usurping" the man's "authority." How I wish I had the exegetical and communication skills to properly explain the true meaning of I Timothy 2:12 as I now understand its true intended meaning by its author, Paul. If I could relive that encounter I would ask this initial question, "Whose authority is being usurped?"

Earlier we spoke about the partnership established by God between Adam and Eve. He also bequeathed to this partnership dominion over all living creatures. After the Fall, in order to protect them from the evil introduced by their fall from grace, God subjected both to roles that would ensure that their marriage survived. She was to be "ruled" by Adam, and she was to be completely focused upon his needs. Adam's sentence (curse) was to be subjected to a life of supporting his family via meaningless, mundane activities carried out to physical exhaustion.

Fast forward to the scene just prior to the Ascension: Jesus bestows on those assembled all power and authority, including casting out unclean spirits as well as heal sickness and disease. [71] But, notice this subtle truth:

the power was given to the church and not to individuals, no matter their position of leadership. On the contrary, the authority to bind and loose people from the power of the Evil One was granted to the church.

In this Great Commission, we discover that this power does not lie as a private treasure of any gender or individual, no matter his or her gender. Rather, as Linda Bellevue pointed out earlier, ". . . it is the church that possesses authority and not particular individuals (or positions, for that matter). It is to the church that Jesus gives the 'keys of the kingdom' (Matt. 16:19) and the authority to 'bind' and 'loose' (that is, enforce and waive, Matt. 18:18)."[72]

So, again we return to the question, whose authority is it in the first place? From what we see in the Scripture it becomes clear that the authority was God's, bestowed by the Son at the end of His triumphant life, and firmly stated in His Word as His to dispense to whomever He determines serves His purpose in establishing His Kingdom and building His Church. This being the case, it is not an authority permanently transferred to any human member of His redeemed community (i.e., the church).

Therefore, how can a woman usurp the authority of a man if that man was never given permanent trust of that authority in the first place. Rather that authority remains in the Word and can be used according to the sovereign will of God as He chooses. Therefore, if He, through the words written by the Apostle Paul, validates the Divine calling and authority of women to ministry, who is to argue that the exercise of such gifts by females is usurpation?

As I recall the Biblical passage discussed in the previous chapter, I realize, afresh, that none of the passages address authority as something from which females are excluded. The issue that Paul zeroed in on, this issue of usurpation as a potential threat to edifying ministry, was important to raise for two reasons.

First, it was raised in order to alert females in ministry leadership that there were constraints imposed by the culture in which the congregation lived to which the leader must adhere, which they must not violate, else they disqualified themselves to be able to access the power of God that would accompany them conducting their ministry with modesty.

The second reason was that the woman leader would not fall into the trap of presenting the message in such a way that she implied that the authority of the message lay in her personality, or skills. Paul, wanted every woman minister to realize that unless the authority of the sermon rests in the integrity of the Word, the result would edify no one. Rather, she must always present the message in such a way that everyone knows that the reason to obey it is that it is the Words given by God, therefore, to be obeyed. This being said, it raises, still, a related question: How does a female leader convey that she is always under authority, and accountable for her words and actions? Permit me to list a few ways.

First, the decision for her selection to leadership was based on the fact that the congregation recognized that she had been divinely given the gifts appropriate for pulpit leadership. This recognition had developed over many years. She probably started out sharing a Bible verse. Then she was given a small role to help guide a discussion group. Next, she was given leadership of a teaching assignment. Later she was trusted with a public ministry, such as I was. Finally, her gifts are abundantly clear to all and she stands as a candidate to be invested with the responsibility for pulpit ministry and guiding a congregation in ministry.

Second, her ministry must be the result of demonstrated "servanthood". Robert Greenleaf first defined a servant leader as a person chosen by the constituency to provide their leadership. In other words, the servant leader serves by leading. This role is the result of a group decision based on their recognition that she possesses the integrity, gifts, vision, and passion to effectively guide their direction. Her leadership is the result of yielding to the will of the congregation, eliminating the hint that she leads by any usurpation. This perfectly describes my journey to leadership. It also describes how I operate, subordinating my will to that expressed by the Holy Spirit through the assembled leadership. Therefore, I base my ministry on my submission to the authority of the Word as the final rule for how I live and what I preach, and my submission to the authority of the corporate leadership of my congregation.

We all meet to pray and seek the mind of Christ as to His will for the direction of our fellowship. I participate in the discussions, and I encourage everyone else to contribute. As a result, a consensus is reached which we ascribe to the Holy Spirit's leading. I would have it no other way. So, where is the usurpation of authority? The idea is nonsense.

Third, a true woman minister with a servant's heart demonstrates her submission in the pulpit in two ways. She shows her yieldedness to the Holy Spirit by limiting her sermon to an explanation of the true interpretation of a Bible text, and tailoring her application to those it reveals (rather than imposing her own will via eisegesis). She also proves her submissive spirit by restricting her use of power (to influence) to that appropriate to her gender—modesty.

Therefore, the female minister is in a pulpit only because her congregation has recognized her gifts, and become convinced of her integrity and vision, that she has been chosen to lead them. So, then, where is the usurpation? It lies only in the minds of those who embrace the Socratic ideas of womanhood and have built a theological defense based on imposing these evil views on certain Biblical verses. It's called eisegesis.

Issue: Headship and "Covering"

Another gender-based 'bump' on the ministry road came when I was denied the help of a male pastor in coordinating a national prayer-mobile. This man, with whom I was acquainted, and considered to be dedicated to Christ, had a proven love for the Lord, and a nationally acclaimed testimony due to his ardent nationwide ministry.

However, he belonged to a vibrant full-gospel denomination that was hesitant to promote women. Unfortunately, I was not aware of that hesitance at the time I appealed to him for his help. But I soon encountered this wall of reluctance when he promptly refused to support my crusade due to what he perceived to be my lack of a 'spiritual covering.' This idea advocates that a woman must not exercise spiritual leadership over any male, since that violates the divinely prescribed hierarchy. I will now review our argument regarding this issue.

J. Lee Grady, author of *10 Lies the Church Tells Women,* points out that "in most cases" the "Leaders have innocently twisted various Bible verses to suggest that a woman's public ministry can be valid only if she is properly 'covered' by a male who is present." [73] Thanks to careful Biblical exegesis, we know such ideas are not supported by any of the proof texts for which those opposed to women preachers reach.

I was fascinated by his report of a prominent fundamentalist leader who, in the 1970s, insisted that single women must remain under the spiritual authority of their fathers until they marry–even if they are responsible adults in their forties or fifties.[74]

This issue of headship actually encompasses two areas. The first area is the issue of whether or not the hierarchy imposed by God is violated when a woman leads men. The second aspect of this issue involves the meaning of Paul's insistence that as she ministers, she does so with a head covering, i.e. the wearing of the veil.

Recall that we looked at the meaning of this Greek word for "head", since that is what Paul wants covered. Its use was meant to convey a metaphor, and to communicate a principle of female leadership related to cultural symbolism. Permit me to explain what I mean by these two ideas, beginning with the use of the word "head" metaphorically.

Also, you will recall, in our analysis of this Greek word we saw, from the context in which it was used, that to Paul, this word translated as "head" served as a metaphor for the place where decisions are made and executed that impacts the direction and well-being of the entire organization. So the first use of the word as a metaphor was to indicate that a spiritual organization, such as a church, does have a decision making center—a hub from which it directs the life of the church.

The second use of the metaphor was in regard to the marriage relationship. To this end, Paul specified a natural hierarchy based on functioning responsibilities: the Head of Christ is God; yet, He is the Head of man, and in turn, man, is the head of woman. This hierarchy was developed to explain how the marriage between the believer and Christ functioned, as well as the earthly marriage between a man and a woman.

So, this hierarchy was divinely set by God and intended for the smooth and successful operation of the marriage relationship. Of course this does spill over into the issue of a woman in pulpit leadership, in that it insists that she must conduct herself in manner and dress in such a way as to not violate her subjection to her husband, and her Lord. To this end, in both cultures (Corinthian and Ephesian) she expressed her subjection to her husband by the wearing of a veil. This leads us to the second aspect of this issue—how the female conducts herself as she provides ministerial leadership of males in the congregation. To appreciate Paul's point, we must look again at the veil as a cultural symbol, and as a metaphor for female leaders.

In the human marriage relationship, the male assumes responsibility to initiate love and provide for his wife's well-being. The woman fulfills her responsibility to the relationship by providing the responding love, and taking responsibility for the nurturing process. The result is a level of intimacy the man declares, according to Paul, as his highest treasure, and becomes the thing that he "glories in". However, this glory is reserved only for the two of them, to be shared at the most intimate level of their relationship. It is not to be brandished about for the public to see; they only need to see that it exists. In every culture, this relationship is expressed by symbolism. In the cultures Paul's writing addressed, it was provided by the wearing of the veil to cover the woman's hair. As the woman's head remained invisible to the eyes of anyone but her husband, so their intimacy was their own special secret.

In modern western cultures it is symbolized by the wearing of a wedding band. Its message was twofold. First, it signified to the watching world, "yes" this intimacy exists, since it is integral to a healthy marriage relationship. Second, it also conveyed this message: "no", like her hair, which is her glory as a woman, no one is permitted to see it but her husband.

However, in Corinth, the prevailing cultures of Corinth and Ephesus used the veil in a way peculiar to the prevailing cultic religions. Since the religious experience involved sexual intercourse with a Temple prostitute, women signaled their availability to service a man by walking about with their hair uncovered.

So when Paul raised the issue in regard to women's role in leading prayer and worship in the public assembly of the Believers, his reason was twofold. First, he wanted the woman to publicly signify that her marriage relationship was healthy, therefore, her submission to her husband in the marital relationship appropriate by the wearing of her veil. It also signified that she was a virtuous woman. So the veil was imperative for any woman called to a prophetic ministry; she must always don the veil to testify her commitment to morality and that, if married, her relationship with her husband was wholesome and consistent with Biblical principles.

Interestingly, men who entered the pulpit to lead in prayer and preach must not wear the veil, even though Paul's own Jewish heritage would have insisted otherwise.

Therefore, does "headship" have any direct bearing on whether a woman can minister or lead males? No, only tangentially; but that relevance to prevailing social mores is important.

Finally, notice that in giving such advice, Paul was tacitly confirming his approval of women for prophetic ministry responsibilities.

Issue: How Can You Preach By Remaining Silent?

You may recall my encounter with a male believer at the Cedros Crusade who tried to silence my preaching of the gospel on the grounds of my gender. Although sincere, he felt compelled to do something about this young female occupying a pulpit in a large assembly where men were present. As mentioned previously, he attempted to reason with me about how wrong it was for a woman to preach where men were present.

Rather than argue with him, I read Joel's prophecy (Acts 2:17-18) and then made my exit, leaving him to meditate on what he had just heard.

Years later I understood why this gentleman confronted me. It occurred as I read the following passage written by Linda L. Belleville, professor of Biblical Literature at North Park Theological Seminary and contributor to *Two Views on Women in Ministry*:

> "One of the continuing hotbeds of debate in evangelical circles today is the nature and scope of leadership roles open to women in the church. Can a woman preach God's word? Can she serve communion, baptize, or lead in worship? Can she marry and bury? Can she serve as the senior or solo pastor? Can she teach an adult Bible class? Can she serve as a bishop, elder, or deacon? Can she put 'Reverend' or 'Pastor' before her name? These are the questions with which numerous churches have struggled and over which some have divided." [75]

Interestingly, after years of this debate raging on, the middle ground on this issue is strangely vacant. No one seems undecided or neutral about it. Yet, detractors continue to rally around what they think is a Biblically sound argument using the four passages we have proven contradict their argument.

The Scriptures place such a high value on believer worship. Hence, Paul counsels those who lead it, including females, to make sure that their efforts render it edifying. This priority is due to two reasons. First, worship fulfills a primary purpose for our regeneration. Doing it right is a matter of great importance to God.

Second, that regeneration results in the Believer obtaining a new spirit. Our new nature is uniquely capable of appreciating and experiencing new emotions such as joy, expressing gratitude which demand outward expression called praise.

Therefore, since edifying worship is such an integral part of the Christian's life, would God insist that half of His redeemed community—the female gender—refrain from praising Him in corporate worship? So the idea that a woman should never express herself in worship is nonsense and cannot be the point of Paul's admonition for the women "to keep silent".

Beyond simple logic, there is another reason to accept this statement: the word that Paul chose for "keep silent". To appreciate Paul's true thinking, one only needs to appreciate the words he had to choose from to express "keep silent" and "speak" in the occurrences of this phrase, (women) "...keep silent" and "...they are not permitted to speak...". They occur in 1 Cor.14:34, and I Timothy 2:11. Paul's selection of Greek words is most enlightening.

To appreciate his choices for the right word to use, let me share them with you:

- *phimoo* (fim-OH-o), which means to muzzle, or force someone to be silent
- *hesuchia* (hey-soo-KEY-ah), means quietness from stillness, (as one might experience while reading a book)
- *Laleo* (lay-LEH-oh), which means, idle chatter, i.e., "chit-chat"
- *Sigao*, (sig-AH-o), represents the kind of silence you might ask, voluntarily, of noisy people assembled in a room, i.e., uttering "Shhhh.", "Shut up, please!"

Actually, there are two occurrences of this admonition for women to "keep silent". Let us deal with both.

In 1 Cor. 14:34, the first instance of the use of this phrase "keep silent", Paul used the word *sigao*. *Sigao* represents the kind of silence you might ask, voluntarily, of noisy people assembled in a room, i.e., uttering "Shhhh.", "Shut up, please!" By choosing this Greek word, he was admonishing people sitting in the audience during worship service to cease from conversations that were disrupting the service thereby spoiling its chances to edify. In 1 Cor. 14:34b -35 Paul qualifies "keep silent" by adding that the women "...are not permitted to *speak...*" and "...it is shameful for women to *speak* ...". His choice of words in both occurrences was *laleo* (idle chatter) and not *phimoo* (forced silence).

His goal was not to muzzle a woman from prophesying, or praying, but women seated in the congregation from making inappropriate, irrelevant conversation that tended to disrupt, e.g., asking aloud questions of their husbands (seated elsewhere). Paul directs his admonition not to women in leadership, but women in attendance.

In the second use of this phrase, "keep silent", in I Timothy 2:11, Paul chose the word *hesuchia*. In this passage he did direct the counsel to "keep silent" to women in ministry leadership. However, this word represents a completely different type of quiet. This word conveys the idea of conducting one's leadership in such a way that your ministry produces a sense of peaceableness (group harmony). Think of his counsel in this way: Do not use your ministry leadership to create disunity and chaos, but rather, make sure that your spiritual admonition is delivered in a spirit that fosters a sense of quietude. How could a female leader prevent chaos that hindered edification? The context supplies the answer.

First, she could foster a peaceable atmosphere by making sure that as she ministered the Word in the pulpit, she did give the impression that her admonition was based on her authority as a leader, and that her power to influence was derived from modesty. Second, she fosters a peaceable atmosphere by making sure she conducted herself in modesty, obeying the rules of custom for a modest female.

Therefore, as you can see the admonition for women to "keep silent" was never intended by the Apostle to muzzle women called to public ministry. Unfortunately, for my Detractors, such clear exegesis is irrelevant. They even have projected their own prejudices about the emotional inferiority of women to argue that their interpretation had to be correct since Paul (like them) was smart enough to realize that women are prone to false doctrine, and even attempt to use the situation of Eve (irrelevant to women in public ministry). They argue that since her sin preceded Adam's, this "proves" why women have invented more false cults than men[76] even though the facts prove otherwise. But when one's mind is made up, what do facts matter?

With regard to women being prone to false doctrine, Tucker and Liefeld said that "this view is not supported by historical fact. On the contrary, it appears that women have traditionally been slower than men to adopt unorthodox theology and to accept the kind of Biblical criticism that undermines the faith."[77]

Mr. Grady expressed a similar view in his book cited previously (*10 Lies the Church Tells Women.*) The point of such 'reasoning', say the Detractors, is that it shows that women are "more prone to deception and must be guarded carefully lest they devise some strange teaching and lead God's people astray."[78] Grady points out that such a view of woman as inherently evil and more easily deceived was not a new idea to the early Church Fathers, but actually a pagan idea inherited from ancient Greek culture, a belief of the 'most revered Greek philosophers' (Socrates).[79]

Detractors also have those they can quote. Grady disagrees with Christian author, David Cloud, who wrote, ". . . It is no coincidence that women have been responsible for starting many of the false Christian movements and have played key roles in Spiritism, New Age, mind science cults and such. . . ."[80]

Unfortunately, Mr. Cloud should have the benefit of the following data from Mr. Grady:

> "Almost every false religion on earth today, in fact, was founded by a man – including Islam, Buddhism and atheistic communism"[81] and that "most of the world's pseudo-Christian cults, such as Sun Myung Moon's Unification Church, were started by men."[82] He said, "Allan Kardec founded the modern spiritist movement; Joseph Smith founded what became the Mormon church; Allister Crowley pioneered an occult religion known as Thelema."[83] Also, we could mention these founders: "Gerald B. Gardner, (modern witchcraft)[84]; L. Ron Hubbard (Church of Scientology); Charles Taze Russel (Jehovah's Witnesses); Mirza Ali Muhammed (Baha'i faith). And Harvey Spencer (Rosicrucians)." [85]

This is not to say that women cannot be deceived or that they cannot invent deceptive philosophies. In fact, they are responsible for three American based cults: Theosophy Society, started by Helena Blavatsky; the Unity movement, founded by Myrtle Fillmore; and the Christian Science movement, established by Mary Baker Eddy.[86]

In truth, the fear of my Detractors regarding Eve was unfounded. The facts show that most of the major religious cults were founded by men.

Conclusion

We close this Section with solid assurance based on Biblical exegesis, and historical data, that women were intended by Jesus and the Apostle Paul for ministry leadership.

We know the source of the idea that women were never intended for such roles, and the sordid motivation for its spread.

So, we leave this discussion knowing that for all the proof available to those who seek to engage in serious debate of this issue offered in Part Two, somewhere it continues to rage as pastors, theologians, and denominational leaders feel it their duty to protect the integrity of the Word that they are convinced makes no allowance for women in leadership. Then, the goal of this discussion was not to change everyone's thinking, only those serious about knowing the truth.

Before us are a host of fascinating characters, women who have populated the record of history as having filled roles of ministry leadership so effectively that they changed the course of church history.

ENDNOTES

68 Ruth A. Tucker & Walter Liefeld, *Daughters of the Church: Women and Ministry from New Testament Times to the Present* (Grand Rapids, Michigan:Zondervan Publishing House, 1987), 16.

69 Ibid.

70 Ibid.

71 Mt 10:1.

72 Beck & Blomberg, 106.

73 J. Lee Grady, *10 Lies the Church Tells Women: How the Bible has been misused to keep women in spiritual bondage* (Lake Mary, Florida: Charisma House, 2000), 89.

74 Ibid. , 90.

75 Linda L. Belleville, Contributor, *Two Views on Women in Ministry,* (Zondervan Publishing House: Grand Rapids, Michigan, 2001), 77.

76 Ibid. , 15.

77 Tucker & Liefeld, 15.

78 Grady, 121.

79 Ibid. , 122.

80 Source obtained from the Internet: David Cloud, "Women Preachers," Fundamentalist Baptist Information Service, Jan. 30, 1998. Quoted in Grady, 122.

81 Grady, 126.

82 Ibid.

83 Ibid.

84 Ibid.

85 Ibid. , 127.

86 Ibid. , 128.

PART THREE
"Church Mothers"
Women of Significant Leadesrship Ministries From Eve to the Modern Era

Is it not refreshing to learn that the record of Scripture is clear: God, the Holy Spirit, never marginalized anyone, based on gender, from ministry leadership?

We know this to be true from sound Biblical analysis of the key verses. Now, we are about to learn from the record produced by twenty centuries of church history, that the Holy Spirit consistently chose women for leadership throughout the history of the church.

Here is the witness of history confirming the correctness of our exegetical conclusions.

Amazingly, this occurred under the ominous shadow of the "Socratic bias" that pervaded the thinking of Church Fathers and Reformers. In such a philosophical climate, male leaders turned to women to perform strategic leadership responsibilities.

Now we shall put faces to these women whose stories make for fascinating reading. To organize material over such a vast amount of time, we shall provide biographies from two broad periods: Biblical era, and Church History era, each organized as its own chapter.

Chapter 8: Biblical Women Leaders

Section One: Eve, Model of all Women in Leadership

Could we find a better model of female leadership than Eve? Actually, the idea to focus upon her life was not ours—the Apostle Paul first introduced it. He properly understood her unique role therefore chose her to support his counsel regarding women in ministry. While we have already dealt with this aspect of Eve in a previous chapter, here we will look at Genesis 2 and 3 to appreciate the relationship between male and female leaders, as modeled by this woman called the "mother of mankind."

Section Two: Female Leaders Ministering in the Old Testament

The faith of Israel was built on the promises made to the Patriarchs. Yet, when it came to ministering to the nation, God also used women spiritually and politically to lead the nation. In this section, we will look at some of the Old Testament women called to leadership and who fulfilled their ministries outstandingly.

Section Three: New Testament Female Leaders Chosen by Jesus and Paul

With Socratic views concerning women firmly entrenched in the Jewish culture, you can appreciate how the Pharisaical leaders were outraged by the way that Jesus chose women for ministering partnerships. In this chapter you will encounter some of the more prominent and interesting females about the Lord's work.

Chapter 9: Women in Church History with Significant Leadership Roles

Since the history of the church is described as that of the Church Fathers, one is surprised by the number of women who fulfilled key leadership roles, often in situations that determined the survival in some strategic situations as well as became the catalyst in the progress of many others.

We have gleaned out biographical vignettes of some of the most interesting women ever called to ministry leadership. To help you keep the historical time straight we will segregate these people into three major eras, each with its own section.

Section One: Pre-Reformation Church History

A hundred years after Paul's writing on women in leadership, Church Fathers reverted to "male only" ministry leadership.

The result was a dark "Socratic cloud" that has since hung over every generation of church history. Yet, in spite of their subjugated role, women stepped up to fulfill key leadership roles, usually with the blessing of male leaders.

Section Two: Women Who Helped Lead the Reformation Movement

As the Reformation dawned, and the problems erupted between governments, cultures and the emerging church, its male leaders turned to females for ministry leadership. If you were to ask men like Luther, Calvin, and John Knox what they thought of women in leadership you would have discovered a strange ambivalence. On the one hand, they espoused a male-only philosophy. Yet they turned to the courageous and capable female leaders you are about to meet for leadership roles.

Section Three: Women Leaders from the Reformation to Modern Twentieth Century

As the Reformation matured and the Protestant church spread to the American colonies, women filled very important leadership positions, especially in turbulent situations. You are about to meet some remarkable women who provided heroic leadership.

Finally, we shine the spotlights on some of the outstanding female ministries in pastoral and missionary roles, including missions.

Prepare now to discover a side of the history of the church that is not often known and therefore little appreciated. You will hear the record of church history crying aloud and clear that…

Women Belong in Leadership!

Chapter 8

Women Leaders in the Bible

It is remarkable how completely the Socratic influence corrupted the thinking of western culture, including many in church leadership. In contrast, however, the Bible never reflects the idea of marginalization of anyone regardless of gender.

We are about to discover how God, in His redemptive story, chose women to play roles strategic to saving and vitalizing their own generation. We have singled out a few examples of females that prove the point (established exegetically in the previous chapters of this book) that God intended for women to serve Him in leadership.

Our goal will be to examine women called by Him to be prophets, judges, and warriors, in order to learn how the female gender functions in leadership. We have selected examples of both Testaments to sample the extent of divine approval of women to serve the Lord in this capacity.

To provide you a map of this discussion, we shall focus on women of the Old Testament in Section Two, and those of the New Testament in Section Three. However, in Section One we will seek to understand the woman who remains the ultimate model of female leadership: Eve, the woman often described as the "mother of humanity".

Section 1: Eve, the Mother of All Female Leaders

Who was Eve and why was she created? The Biblical answer to this question is critical to understanding the nature and function of all women. In this section, we shall understand the answers to these questions and more.

A thorough and careful study of the first three chapters of the book of Genesis is crucial to understanding the nature and function of the first woman, Eve. To this end we will analyze the narrative for clues as to why she was created, starting with the reason God created *them* and placed *them* in the Garden of Eden, beginning with the creation of Adam.

God's Purpose in Creating Adam

After the creation of the heavens, earth, and its component forms of life, God took the man (*adam*) that he had created, "(and) put him in the Garden of Eden to work it and take care of it" (Gen. 2:15).

Shortly into his mission, as he noted that the animals he named had mates, Adam realized that he had none. Noting this, the LORD God said, "It is not good that man should be alone; I will make him a helper comparable to him" (Gen. 2:18). After pronouncing everything good that He made, we suddenly find that God views Adam's loneliness as a bachelor as unacceptable.

Therefore, the Lord moves to correct this inadequacy by creating him "a helper of comparable status". The phrase means that Eve would be an equal partner in status, but with different skills and perspective in approaching her assignments. The exciting discovery before us in a study of this Genesis narrative is how God made Eve a partner so different from the way in which natural man views a helper, i.e., "a subordinate role for one with inferior skill competency".

This commonality is described in the following verse:

> And God said, "Let us make MAN in our image, in our likeness, and let THEM rule over the fish of the sea and the birds of the air, over the livestock, over all the earth, and over all the creatures that move along the ground." So God created man in His own image, in the image of

> God he created him; MALE and FEMALE he created them (emphasis mine) [(Gen. 1:26, 27].

As I point out several important exegetical clues, you will see that both genders were in the mind of God as equal in status.

Clue #1

Notice that the singular word "man" is supported by a plural pronoun "them". In Hebrew grammar, the pronoun must be of the same person and case of the noun it modifies. What is the point of this strange grammatical construction? How can the singular noun, *adam*, be grammatically rectified with the plural pronoun, "they"? The key lies in understanding the meaning of the Hebrew word translated "adam".

The word "*adam*" is not a name, but a noun representing a class of creation—humankind. Alvera Mickelsen points out that "...the Hebrew word *'adam'* is sometimes used in the sense of humankind, as in these verses (Gen. 1:26-28); sometimes as the name for an individual, as in Genesis 2; sometimes for Adam and Eve together, as in Genesis 5:3".[87]

So the answer to the question about whom this word is referring to is this: The '*Adam*' is a 'they.' This can be proven by the fact that the clause, 'he created him', is connected to the clause that follows it in the next sentence, "he created them" , by a Hebrew grammatical device (called 'parallelism'). Since *Adam the man* cannot be both a male and a female, this word, '*adam,*' can only be logically translated as 'human' or 'humanity.'[88]

Clue #2

Now observe a second grammatical clue that supports this understanding of the word '*adam*' as humankind. This Hebrew word '*adam*' is preceded by the definite article. When the Jewish scholars translated this word into Greek in the Septuagint, they chose the Greek equivalent word for this unique construction, *anthropos*. Perhaps you recall, from our previous investigation of this Greek word (chapters 6 and 7) that we compared it to its close synonym, the Greek word, *aner*. You will remember that we said that the word *aner* means an individual who is a member of the male gender. In contrast, *anthropos* is a word that is gender-inclusive, i.e., includes all human beings. Therefore, the first use of the term *man* refers to *humankind* rather than solely to the male species.

Clue #3

Notice the nature of their calling: both are to "rule" over the creation. The word *rule* in the Hebrew, *Masal*, means "to rule, reign; to have dominion."[89] English synonyms of the word *rule* are govern, run, administrate, have power over, lead, control, preside over, and direct. But the Bible declares that both male and female were given authority by the Creator to jointly rule, contradicting the idea (popularized by Socrates) that men were divinely intended to rule i.e., dominate women.

Having established the fact that they were created equal in their purpose, did the Fall impact this? Yes, to the headship that was divinely established at the outset, under the curse, this further condition was added to the woman: ". . . your desire will be for your husband, and he will rule over you" (Genesis 3:16). That subordination would have remained today (as my Detractors insist) except for one thing: the Cross! Jesus, for the work of building His kingdom, reinstated both genders to their former positions in Christ (Romans 3:24).

Clue #4

Notice that to cement this partnership God gave them three incredible means of bonding them into a unity. This unity was so complete that Adam describes it as if Eve was his own flesh and bone. First, God took her out of Adam's side so that he could never again think of her as different from himself, and therefore, would have to deal with her as if blessing her was the only way he could be blessed. Second, physical intimacy joined them into a single unit in a way that Paul said is a mystery. Third, God 'dressed' them in "nakedness without shame". That Hebrew phrase "naked without shame" suggests more than nudity. It conveys the sense of being totally open and exposed as a person before God and man. It means they had nothing to be rightly ashamed of, nothing to hide. Surely, this enabled them to enjoy perfect communication (Gen. 2:24-25).

Clue #5

The phrase, "a helper comparable to me," is a gold mine of insight into the nature of their partnership, especially as we examine each word. To this end, we will use the English equivalent of each word in this phrase, which could be translated as "help-meet".

Key Word: "Helper"

In modern times, people have come to understand the meaning of 'help' in the sense of serving as a maid or domestic servant, which is universally regarded as a subordinate position. For the original meaning of the phrase, "help meet," let us turn to the Hebrew.

The Hebrew word for "help," which some Biblical scholars translate as "partner," is *'ezer.* In secular literature, this word is used to mean, "to render help as a military ally" would. When God is spoken of as our 'helper,' we are really speaking of Him as our strength or power."[90] To augment this sparse insight, we only need to use the hermeneutical tool to locate the word being used in other Biblical passages in order to gain a fuller composite understanding of the word's intended meaning. I will look at three Biblical verses.

First, observe how Moses used the word in this passage: "My father's God was my helper (*'ezer*); he saved me from the sword of Pharaoh" (Ex. 18:4). Here the word carries the idea of help as essential as life itself.

Next, notice how the Psalmist used this word: "I will lift up my eyes to the hills. Where does my help (*'ezer*) come from? My help (*'ezer*) comes from the LORD, the Maker of heaven and earth" (Ps. 121:2). Here, the word is connected to the man's hope. Because we know that hope is the most essential need of the human species, this certainly elevates the idea of "helper" to something as essential as one's emotional well-being.

From these verses, we learn two things about this word *'ezer* (translated 'helper'). First, it is never used as something provided by a subordinate.

This truth is supported by the second observation that this "help" is most often delivered by God. Would my Detractors think of "help(er)" as secondary or subordinate in that context?

Key Word: "Meet"

Now we look at the second word in the key phrase, "help meet", the Hebrew word translated as "comparable", *kenegdo*, which means "equal and corresponding to."[91] It can mean nothing else than that Eve, as a partner, was equal in every way to Adam.

R. David Freedman, Biblical scholar and specialist in Semitic languages, after thoroughly examining all possible uses of this phrase in the Old Testament concluded that the correct translation for Genesis 2:18 should be: 'I will make a power (or strength) equal to him.' [92]

Adam and Eve then, were made equal partners, designed to work together in partnership with each other to rule the earth. Eve complemented Adam, was comparable to him, and the result was they were both blessed. God even pronounced it "as very good."[93]

The textual evidence from this passage of Genesis can lead to only one conclusion: God created both genders equally in his "image" and "likeness" and bonded them together so that they can only jointly rule over creation. Eve was to be such an intimate partner that Adam could only find blessing as he blessed her.

Like the argument of how many angels can dance on the head of a pin, I find the debate among psychologists as to the differences between the genders to be like arguing about the difference between ice and steam, i.e., one being superior to the other.

To me the larger point is that they are both forms of water; they serve a common purpose only in different ways.

Regarding their differences, as leaders, I have found enlightening insight by analyzing the Hebrew words that describe their relationship to humanity, i.e., "father" and "mother".

The Hebrew language was originally designed as pictures that when strung together formed a coherent idea. Let me illustrate. Years ago, while visiting the US, I discovered a popular bumper sticker that used this same kind of "sign language". It formed a message from three symbols: an *eye* plus a *heart* plus the letters *NY*. When decoded it meant, "I love New York." I was impressed by the way this use of simple pictures could convey an idea using a minimal amount of space yet which could be quickly understood. I then reflected on the way in which the Hebrew language uses letters in a similar way. Let me explain.

The Hebrew language was one of the first languages to convert picture symbols to letter symbols. For example, let us look at the original Hebrew word for "walk." The original word combined two pictographic symbols (letters) to form an essential idea of its meaning. The two letters are "lamed" and "kaph". First, let me explain the meaning of each letter. The "lamed" is a shepherd's staff. This staff was the constant companion of every shepherd and male who was walking. It provided both support and protection. The second letter pictured an open hand with fingers outstretched. When combined, these two letters represented a person using a staff, since the hand was curved about it to hold it up. The resulting word formed meant "to walk", since no man ventured to walk without carrying his staff.

As you can see, the two letters made a composite picture that resembled the meaning of the word they formed. Now let us apply this knowledge to understanding the meaning of "father" and "mother."

Father: ab (Hebrew "AB")

The Hebrew word for "father" is the word AB ("ahb"). It is formed of two letters. We will now examine each of these to understand the meaning of "father" embraced by the Hebrew language.

Aleph ("A")

The "A" was originally a picture of an Ox. In fact, if you turn an English capital letter "A" upside down you will see a facsimile of this symbol, since we get our letter from this original letter. So what did the Hebrew symbol mean? They considered the Ox as a very important animal. It was certainly the strongest domesticated animal in their pasture. Its strength was their chief form of transporting goods from one place to another. Its meat was used at major celebrations. Its hide was used for leather. Also, it was the most important sacrificial animal since its sacrifice could provide the blood to cleanse an entire nation of sin.

Beth (B)

The Hebrew letter "Beth" is equivalent to our letter *b*. In fact, if you turn a capital letter "B" sideways you will see a rough facsimile of its shape. The shape of this letter represented the floor-plan of the Hebrew tent made of goat skins. It was divided into two sections, one for the males and the other for females.

When one combines these two letters, the result presents a fascinating insight into the Hebrew concept of fatherhood. A father was viewed as the source of power and strength since he supports the entire family as the center pole does in the tent. This Center-pole was also sharpened at one end so it could be stuck into the ground for stability when the tent was raised. So the center pole could also be used as a weapon (spear) to protect the family.

So the Hebrew concept of a father is one who is at the center of the family providing its protection, support, strength, and structure. As previously discussed, a male leader also brings these qualities to those he serves.

Now let us look at the Hebrew word for "mother": "AM" ("ahmm"). This Hebrew word was also comprised of two letters. The first one, "Aleph," we have already looked at. It signifies that she will be considered a source of strength, structure, protection, and support, although in a different way from her spouse. The second letter, "M" ("mmm"), determines the difference. The letter drew meaning from two metaphors.

The first metaphor from which it derived meaning was as a picture of waves of water on a large body of water, i.e. Mediterranean Sea with two arms curling about something the sea holds up, i.e., a ship. The ship represents the family, which the mother holds together by her loving arms. The Sea represents the place into which the setting sun sinks. So mother is the leadership that holds the family together as it moves into the future (tomorrow).

The second metaphor is useful to describe how she holds the family together. To the Hebrew, the strongest liquid was glue. It was manufactured by boiling hides. The viscous liquid glue that rose to the top was skimmed off. That glue was useful to hold any two objects together.

The picture that emerges from these alphabet symbols: the mother leads the family by providing the strength that bonds all into a common unity and supports them by the love that comes from within her so that they need not fear the future. It is a nurturing type of leadership.

Is it not amazing how just the names of "father" and "mother" instruct us as to the interactive nature of male and female leadership, whether in the family or church ministry? The male leader provided the strength and support as a center pole in a family tent, and the female provide the strength and support by holding the interior together in her arms that enfolded and held it together for the future like glue.

Section 2: Women Leaders in the Old Testament

At the outset, we face a paradox between the treatment of women outside the Bible, and their usefulness as described within its narrative.

The religious leaders treated the female species as chattel. Listen to a well known Rabbi Eliezer:

> "Rather should the words of the Torah be burned than entrusted to a woman. Whoever teaches his daughter the Torah is like one who teaches her obscenity".

This religious prejudice carried over into almost every aspect of most women's lives:

- Women were confined to the homes of their fathers or husbands
- Women, being inferior to men, were forced to live under the direct authority of their fathers before marriage and their husband until death
- Women were not allowed to testify in court trials
- Women could not appear in public venues
- Women could not talk to strangers

- Women were required to be doubly veiled when venturing outside their homes

The glaring truth is women in ancient Israel had a status, not unlike that of women in Afghanistan, during the grossly oppressive rule of the Taliban.

On the other hand, women who were contemporaries of the patriarchs, prophets, and poets fulfilled leadership roles without any restriction.

I cannot reconcile this terrible dichotomy. I can only report how women from Sarah to the prophet, Anna, the last Old Testament female leader (who actually gazed into the face of the baby Jesus) contributed with their leadership. We shall focus on these outstanding women, plus five other stellar personalities: Jochebed, Miriam, Deborah, Jael, and Huldah.

True, they represent only a small contingent of the host of women who filled leadership positions during the "Old Covenant" era. But they all share one thing; they prove that God considered their appointment as vital to His purpose, and put His hand upon them to draw them into leadership ministries.

1. Sarah: Wife of the Father of the Faith

Many Bible scholars feel that the history of salvation begins in Genesis chapter 12. As Adam is the father of humanity, Abraham is the father of the race of regenerated humanity. So God's call to Abraham was as important as Adam's birth.

Paul, in Romans 4, makes this a key point of his argument regarding the faith that God accepts to grant access to His Presence, establish a vital personal relationship on earth, and access to His heaven.

Viewed from another perspective, we see the importance of Abraham by the esteem in which three major world religions - Christianity, Judaism, and Islam - revere him. They all consider his faith as a model for their own constituents.

Certainly, this elevates the leadership role of Sarah, because throughout all of Abraham's life, as we know of it, he was a married man. Therefore, Sarah was half of one of the most important leadership teams in redemptive history. Peter pointed out this fact; Sarah, since she was the mother of the promised seed, became the mother of all believers.

Think about how miraculous it was that she was the one in succession to give birth to a son, and through him, ultimately to the Messiah. Abraham is the seventh son of Noah. After hundreds of thousands of offspring, the Messianic hope resided in this single couple: a husband nearing a hundred years of age, and a wife long past the child-bearing age and barren.

How do their respective roles demonstrate how a partnership between female and male leadership functions? Think of Abraham as exemplifying the model for "Begetting". In balance, I shall call Sarah's role that of a "Bearer".

With Abraham and Eve, God changes the nature of His relationship to the Godly. They defined the nature of the kind of faith that God accepts to grant salvation.

A cursory study of one of the key passages on faith in the New Testament confirms how important faith is to salvation: "By grace are you saved, through faith. It is the gift of God unto salvation" (Eph. 2:8, 9). What does that pronoun, "it" refer to? I can assure you that syntactically, it modifies the word "faith".

Since faith is so important to becoming a true believer, the first couple to model it so that everyone else could understand and utilize it makes the role of Sarah and Abraham very important.

What was Sarah's role in modeling this saving faith? Since her story spans so many chapters of Genesis, we will only cull out incidents that focus on her calling as a partnering leader. The first instance involves her first act of partnering leadership.

i. Sarah's Leadership at the "Call"

Abraham's call was also his wife's, since they were "one in the flesh".

His leadership, responding to God's call to leave Ur and set out for the Land of Promise, provides us a good model of an important characteristic of male leadership—taking initiative.

Her leadership, like glue, lay in the way she kept the life of their family intact as the caravan proceeded into unknown territory. At the outset, she is conscious of her husband's integrity; therefore, embraces God's call to her husband as her own calling. I have exercised this kind of leadership many times. For example, I am attending a Board meeting of our congregation, and the revealed will of God becomes clear through the consensus reached after much discussion on an issue of importance to the direction and wellbeing of our church family.

In such instances, I subordinate my will to that which has been shown to be the determined will of God. In like manner, Sarah exercised true servant leadership by her acceptance of God's will revealed through her husband.

ii. Sarah's Leadership in Egypt

When they moved into Egypt, Abraham's half-truth has created a terrible mess. Yet, Sarah saved their lives and kept alive the Messianic hope by speaking with the Pharaoh with honesty, and faith that God would move him to respond in grace. To me, this incident proves that God's work is best served by partnerships formed by leaders of both genders making it possible for one to do what the other cannot.

iii. Birth of Ishmael

In the horrible attempt to fulfill the Messianic promise by a contrived gimmick, both she and Abraham showed bad judgment, and a complete lack of faith. As the boy's presence threatens their family's future, Sarah exercised true leadership by demanding that the boy and his mother must both leave the compound and never return. When Abraham whines, God says, Sarah's judgment is correct and that he must acquiesce to her leadership. Could there be any clearer confirmation of the legitimacy of her call to leadership?

iv. New Names

From the new names God gave them, we learn another insight into the uniqueness of female and male leadership. Abraham's new name would no longer be, "Father of Many" (i.e., the head of a large family) but "Father of Many Nations". The meaning: out of all nations, people who exercise their faith in the Messiah like Abraham did, would become a covenant people—a spiritual nation that encompassed every country, tribe and people group.

But notice the new name given to Sara—Sarah. It means "princess". Her original name was "Sara" which means "princely one"; i.e., a woman who has such an exquisite face and figure to be worthy of marrying a prince. This new name marked her as true royalty, i.e., a mother whose son would sit on a Throne. This name also shows that God considered her a full partner in joint-leadership. This new name did become a fulfilled prophecy. Her grandson, Jacob, after his deep spiritual encounter with YHWH at Bethel, did receive a new name—Prince with God. So this princess did give birth to a prince.

v. Staring at Moriah

Do you think that when Abraham packed firewood, a knife, and took the hand of his young son that she was not aware of the magnitude of this venture? Her hope was bound up in the son she had brought forth from her womb. Since Moriah was visible in the distance from their starting place, I have no doubt the woman stared at that distant mountain desperate for what God would do. Yet from it, her faith became fully New Testament mature—she saw the promise of life in God's promise as extending through death to the resurrection.

In closing, permit me to share with you my reflections regarding her strategic importance as the "Bearer" and nurturer. Sarah becomes a catalyst to provide many insights into how female leadership nurture true faith. We see it in her submission to known will as expressed through Abraham, at times, and at other times, taking the helm to provide the direction to safety for them both. We see it in the way she guides the promise made to her husband to fruition by correcting the results of bad judgments. We see it in the way she nurtures Isaac from infant to manhood.

Where did this woman gain such insight into the life of believing faith? It grew out of exercising her gift of maternal leadership. It emerged as she and her husband jointly struggled to live in obedience to the calling, embraced the promise as their own, and built their lives about the resulting relationship. As a result, in Sarah, we see a leader on par with Eve. Eve was the mother of humanity; and Sarah, the mother of regenerated humanity.

2. Mother of the Deliverer

As Eve was the mother of mankind, and Sarah, the mother of saved mankind, so Jochebed became the mother of the man who would transform Sarah's family into a nation.

Jochebed's claim to fame lies in the unique role she had in preserving the life of her infant son, Moses. As a result, she shared in the blessing and spiritual reward of everything that her son accomplished, because without her leadership efforts, he would have died at birth.

Therefore, because of Jochebed, the rat-tag descendants of Jacob arose from slavery to enjoy the abundant existence in the land promised to Abraham. They also gained a complete understanding of how to walk with the God of the Patriarchs, thanks to the Torah her son wrote, and Tabernacle he built.

A Model of Leadership Principles

The story of this sainted mother's actions serves as a case study for a management course in college of what a leader does. To this end, permit me to point out how her actions were consistent with those of a true leader.

Principle One: Leadership must Proceed from the Heart

Her name offers an important clue to her relationship with God: Jochebed means, "glorifying Yahweh is my most important value". Surely, the woman's life demonstrates that she lived up to her name.

Principle Two: Spiritual Leadership Requires Covenant Relationship

She was a direct descendant to Abraham through his grandson Jacob, as well as Jacob's son Levi, and Levi's son Kohath, born in his senior years.

Kohath was her older brother. He bore a son, Amram, whom Jochebed married, making her an aunt of her husband's.

This strange intergenerational connection served an important purpose.

Later, the spiritual community which Moses led would be shepherded by the descendants of Levi; and her other son, Aaron, would be its first High Priest, and begin the succession of people to this office through his sons and grandsons. Without the complete purity of that Levitical line, the nation could not have enjoyed the close relationship it had via the offerings and Tabernacle worship. As then, spiritual leadership can only proceed from a covenant relationship through a genuine new-birth experience, and a sustained relationship with God that flows from a whole-hearted commitment to walk before Him as the pre-requisite to serving Him.

Principle Three: Experience Matters

She was also an older woman when Moses was born, since the Biblical record shows that her father Levi lived to a very old age, and she was advanced in years at the birth of Moses. Therefore, she is a true bridge between the Patriarchs that preceded the Captivity and the nation that marched out of Egypt into the Promised Land. Truly, she was the glue between the generations that followed her son into the desert and all that began with Abraham and Sarah.

Anatomy of True Leadership

Permit me to point out principles we can learn from her leadership.

1. Correct Perception of the Situation

The Pharaoh came to the throne determined to "be his own man". He felt no compunction to respect or reward the Jews for the good things that Joseph had done to rescue the nation from seven years of terrible famine.

As Pharaoh watched God prosper the Jews in the remote border region of Goshen, he felt that these farmers and ranchers presented an enormous threat, not by overthrowing his government, but by joining forces with an invading neighbor seeking to remove him from his throne.

To that end, he used his power to slow down the births of newborn sons. However, God thwarted his plan, using courageous Jewish midwives. Then he turned to violence dispatching squads of military thugs to invade homes, grab small boys, and drown them in the Nile.

People follow leaders they trust. That trust is based upon followers' perception that the leaders know what they are doing. They reach this conclusion by being shown a solid plan of action for that problem's solution. In this Jochebed proved herself a true leader.

2. She Caught a Vision of How to Solve the Problem

After the birth of her third son, the edict to drown male infants in the Nile reached her house. The two older children, Miriam, and younger brother, Aaron, had both been born before the edict to kill the boy babies. Moses, a very beautiful infant, was born with a death sentence upon his head.

3. She Developed a Strategic Plan

Her idea was to hide the boy; but after only three months, that plan failed. Therefore, like a true leader she improvised, developing a "Plan B". She constructs a water-tight container amid the weeds in the Nile River near her home. Since crocodiles populated the river, she needed to minimize the time the infant was afloat. She calculated the very moment that the Pharaoh's daughter bathed in the Nile. Jochebed's hope was that this beautiful baby boy would catch this woman's eye, and move her heart to adopt the boy, saving him from certain death. She stationed her daughter, Miriam, who was not a child, where she could watch over Moses, and be there to instruct Pharaoh's daughter, should the Lord move her heart to take the boy. This was a woman of faith; a leader capable of conceiving and executing a well thought out plan. As I learned in a graduate course on Strategic Planning, nothing happens without this kind of carefully thought out blueprint.

Sure enough, the plan came to pass! The young Egyptian girl not only became infatuated with this Hebrew infant, she agreed to raise it in the palace. Then, remarkably, when Miriam suggested she could find a "Nanny" to watch over the lad, the princess ordered her to bring the woman (who was, in fact, his natural mother). Jochebed got to raise her son until he could eat solid food, and the world gained a man who changed it as few had before him, or since.

Imagine YHWH calling and gifting this woman for such a strategic leadership position!

Lessons

What lessons can we learn from Jochebed that will help us better understand the special kind of leadership that females execute so well?

- Faith, vision, strategic planning, and execution are everything. The size of the responsibility matters little.
- Leadership must not be measured by its position on the organizational chart.
- Judge good leadership by the way, in the worst of situations, with only what is available, the leader delivers with no concern for her personal welfare.
- Execution is, in the end, everything; leadership must be held accountable for results not just its ability to see a need.
- Faith plus work beats faith alone.

This woman, at a most critical moment, became the catalyst to rescue millions of people from terrible abuse and bondage, simply by responding to a problem by faith and a trust in God that superseded her concern for her own personal safety.

Bottom line, Jochebed proved to be an exceptional leader. Small wonder that God chose her for such a strategically important task; giving birth to not only the Deliverer, Moses, but also its first High Priest, Aaron, as well as the first female Poet and Prophet, Miriam.

3. First Female Prophetic Voice

The role Miriam played in early Hebrew history was revealed by the prophet, Micah. Speaking through Micah to the children of Israel, the Lord said, "I brought you up out of Egypt and redeemed you from the land of slavery. I sent Moses, Aaron and Miriam." (Mic. 6:4, NIV).

Think about those words; centuries after her death, a true prophet, under the inspiration of the Holy Spirit, reveals that after all that time, Israel still revered her as a true female leader. Micah's words confirm the fact that God chose this female as His first prophetic preacher to the nation.

True, pride caused momentary failure; but that must be balanced against decades of faithful ministry.

As we track her life, we discover insights into how female leadership emerges, and how its responsibilities can change.

Insights

Leaders Emerge

Miriam illustrates this important point about leadership (male and female): Leaders do not spring from behind a bush fully mature, trained, and ready to take charge. I chose her because she beautifully models female leadership in emergence.

We first see Miriam as a young girl (although no child) standing guard over her youngest brother, floating naked in a small craft/basinet, in the Nile, a river infested with crocodiles, and responding to the request of Pharaoh's daughter.

In this early incident, we see her proactive leadership skills showing evidence as an emerging leader. Face it, her quick wittedness, and sensitivity to the Lord, saved the day not just for her infant brother, Moses, but also for her entire family.

Leadership is Forward Focused

Later, as Moses began his leadership as the Savior of the Israelites from Egyptian bondage, it became clear that this was not a rescue from Egypt, but a calling into a new relationship with God. The descendants of Jacob would become the nation bearing his divinely called name, Israel. Suddenly the promises made to Abraham and Sarah moved into a new dimension. The princess (Sarah) finally had the heir she was called to bear, and he was a nation!

Female Leadership Works Well with "Being"

What role did her leadership gel into, finally? Her ministry was to provide leadership for the worship, led by her brother Aaron, according to the written design revealed to her brother Moses by God as a perfect model of His nature and work in salvation. Her calling was not to guide the nation across the Sinai, but to make sure that, while enroute, Israel lived for God as His Covenant People. Is it not revealing that her brother, Moses, explains that God gave her some of the direct revelation that became part of the Torah (Numbers 12:1-2)? Here we see the feminine touch to leadership. She motivates them to become who they were meant to be; she develops strategies that reflect intelligent planning, she handles her pulpit responsibilities with words that touches the heart with the warmth of music.

Miriam perfectly models the emerging female leader that ultimately becomes the first prophetic voice for God to the nation.

4. The Bee Who Became Her Honor, the Queen

Within a generation of the death of Joshua, the nation he helped birth was on the ropes. A nation that had enjoyed a century of Godly direction slid from a theocracy led by able high priests, and Godly statesmen, to a federation of Tribal fiefdoms controlled by cousins.

Meanwhile, the Canaanite nations that Joshua had defeated, and whose land and possessions these millions of cousins now possessed, were now re-armed and mad enough to spill blood to recapture it.

Israel, like a bee hive was coming apart again, for the fourth time. After three male leaders, God, on this occasion, chose a woman, Deborah. Her name, in Hebrew, means a 'bee'. Think of the qualities we credit to the bee: industry, sagacity, teamwork, sense of self-sustaining community. This 'bee", from the Tribe of Benjamin, was about to become the "Queen' who saved the national hive.

Moses had established this office of "Judge". Deuteronomy 17:9 describes a position of power that functioned alongside that of the high priest, only in non-liturgical and spiritual matters.

Both Moses and Joshua filled this position. Now this able woman was Divinely chosen to fill the position. The technical term for this type of government is "Gynaecocracy", i.e., a government ruled by female leadership.

While she held the title of "Judge", technically, she functioned as a prophet, but people perceived her prophetic utterances as judicial decisions. Interestingly, she introduced a genre of prophetic ministry that resembled the format of the psalms. Later prophets would modify this by combining a narrative of a vision shown to them, shaped into a sermonic format, with some poetical expression included. Think about that: a female preacher first shaped the prophetic ministry!

Deborah was called a "judge". The Hebrew word, '*shephet*', means "to set erect". She set up court under a tree, and people throughout the land lined up for her to arbitrate both civil and criminal matters. Suddenly, thanks to a mighty neighboring army led by a very able General, Sisera, a major region of Israel was threatened with slavery and ruin.

Notice this able leader's decisiveness. First, she proclaims a word of hope and encouragement to those staring into this ugly future. Then she appointed an able General, a man named Barak, to form an army of ten thousand and prepare to conquer Sisera, and the army of a king whose name was Jabin.

Barak agrees on one condition: she must accompany him to the battlefield. The reason, according to a leading theologian, Franz Delitschz, was that the man lacked sufficient confidence in his own spiritual power. Deborah scolds him and declares that the victory will come to pass as she had predicted, but, thanks to his lack of confidence, he will not get the credit—it will fall to a woman, Jael.

Therefore, this man turned to this female leader to supply him with the spiritual strength as he marched into battle. So much for passive female leadership—here is a woman turned warrior, right in the midst of the action on the battlefield (Judges 4:12-16).

The Bee is about to plant a very large stinger into the skull of General Sisera, thanks to the hands-on work of another woman, Jael. As a result, the enemy king, Jabin, and his kingdom were destroyed.

What was her role? First, she confirmed the promises of the Lord to Abraham, and Moses. Listen to her war cry: "Has not the Lord of Israel commanded?" Surely, here is an excellent illustration of God putting His spirit upon a woman in leadership in order to convey His will for their future.

Next, she delivered a "Song" that conveyed incredible hope. It describes the impending victory as the work of God was executed to fulfill His promises made to Israel via Abraham.

She demanded that everyone direct all rejoicing to YHWH, since He would be the One to turn

the impending disaster into victory, death into life, and restore national life to a state of well-being similar to a well-working "Hive" again.

In "her Honor, Deborah," the role of female leadership moves from strictly spiritual ministry to that of national prominence.

5. The Librarian Who Saved Josiah's Reign with a Book

It is axiomatic that whenever the Bible gets "rediscovered", i.e., restored to its legitimate place of authority as the very words of God for the true believers, revival breaks out.

In two brief Bible passages, 2 Kings 22 and 2 Chronicles 34, we meet a very special woman who lit the fire of revival for the last time in Israel before its final fragmentation. After generations of failure, Israel was about to enjoy one last respite from the slide toward captivity under Nebuchadnezzar.

Josiah was the son of a despicable king of Israel. Due to the man's death, Josiah assumed the throne while a small boy. As he grew into manhood, God moved Josiah's heart to want to lead the people according to the will of God. He ordered the renovation of the Temple built by his great, great grandfather, Solomon, to encourage worship. In the process, workmen discovered two treasures hidden in the walls of the old building; a large amount of offering funds that had been squirreled away for safe-keeping, and an ancient manuscript they barely recognized, the Torah.

The High Priest asked King Josiah what was his pleasure to do with these items. The King asked the man to read the Torah to him. As the High Priest reached the part that told of the nation's impending doom if it did not follow God's commands and bring its life under His sovereign will, the Lord touched the king's heart with true repentance. The king, in shock, tore his clothes, and jumped up as if shot at. What a testimony to the power of the Word of God to trigger revival when it is communicated under the anointing of the Holy Spirit.

Josiah, fascinated by this "Book of the Law", asked his close advisor, Ahikam, to recommend someone who could explain its meaning to him. This advisor could have turned to Jeremiah (who was his close friend) or Zephaniah. After all, the writings of these two prominent prophetic voices ended up in the Old Testament. Nevertheless, the Lord directed this man to turn to a woman. Her name was Huldah. She was the royal librarian, but the incident transformed her into a prophet.

Huldah was the wife of a man close to the king since he managed his royal wardrobe. She was the librarian of the main college that trained priests, government workers, and legal minds. It was located in a building complex adjacent to the Palace.

Because of her knowledge of books, and this one in particular, Ahikam approached her to explain the Prophetic words written in the Scroll. As she began this task, the Spirit of the Lord came upon her and she approached the king in an uncharacteristic manner. Using ordinary royal protocol, she should have used verbiage like this: "O Mighty King, it is a great honor to be able to advise you in this manner, oh sovereign…"

Instead, she speaks with authority, as if the very words of God were hers, "Tell that man…" Why did she address her king as "that man"? Because these words were from the mind and heart of the living God, and to Him, a king was no different from anyone else. Her counsel changed the course of the nation.

Then she announced, under the anointing of the Holy Spirit, that the words the king had heard were from God and meant for Jerusalem. She explained that this judgment was for the idolatry that had been practiced by the king's father. She then confronted the High Priest for the sin of tacitly allowing this wickedness to exist. Finally, she offered the king a message of hope, i.e., that God was going to spare Josiah from the crushing destruction of the Babylonian army, because of his sincere repentance, and his desire to lead the people in a direction that pleased the Lord.

How's that for candor! Ordinarily, that might have gotten a person beheaded, except, everyone present recognized that the woman speaking to them was a true prophet anointed by God.

Her name is illuminating: "Huldah" means "the Mole". This connection was significant. As a mole stores away things so that they endure, she had been storing away the scrolls that contained the Words of Life. She, during those times, had been studying them. Therefore, when the proper time arrived, God tapped her to fill a very important leadership position.

Once again, we see, the sovereign hand of Jehovah, bypassing capable, Godly, competent male leadership to draft a woman for His purpose. As a result, she became the Instructor of the King, and thereby, a catalyst into bringing decades of well-being to the nation of Israel as its leader, and under her tutelage, led it to a day of spiritual vitality.

Miriam helped Moses lead the people out of Egypt. Deborah led them from the brink of disaster. Huldah, a true female prophet of God, gave Israel a final season of peace and blessing.

6. Prophetic Last Word of the Old Testament

Imagine, three hundred years after Malachi's prophetic words fell into silence, God had one final statement to make to Israel, especially to those true believers who had lived in obedience to His promise of a Messiah, known as the "Remnant". For this last word before His Son came to speak for Himself, God chose a woman for a last prophetic word.

I find it ironic that this elderly, saintly woman whom we call "Anna", ("Hannah" by her contemporaries), delivered a message of hope with the source of that hope cradled in her arms.

The newborn infant, Jesus, was at the Temple because his parents desired to obey the Mosaic law that every first born son had to be dedicated to Him. To comply with this law, the boy could be devoted to the Lord and left at the Temple to be reared by its Levitical staff, or a small offering could be made to "redeem" him so he could be raised by his parents at home.

As Mary and Joseph make their offering, a man named Simeon begins to prophesy about the future of Jesus and extols him as the true Messiah. He praises God that he has lived to see with his own eyes the Messiah promised in the Garden of Eden. Here, in humble swaddling clothes lays the Prince promised to Abraham and Sarah, the Royal Son promised to David who would take the throne and occupy it until the end of time and beyond. The man's eloquence and spirit soared; as a result, a crowd gathered to see the source of this commotion.

Suddenly at his side was the woman he had known for decades. Her heart also bursts with the realization that, in this baby, prophecy was being fulfilled. Suddenly, as Simeon finishes, she breaks out with her own prophetic utterance. Her anointed message was directed at the spiritual minority in Jerusalem who had steadfastly lived in conformity to the Word, always in constant, abiding expectation that the Messiah would appear since the Old Testament prophets had promised.

Who was this woman? She was a widow, just past either her 84th birthday, or approaching her 103rd, depending on how you interpret Luke's statement regarding her widowhood. She had grown up in Galilee. She was of the Tribe of Asher. You may recall Asher was the son of Zilpah, a Cushite woman, therefore, Anna was probably a woman of color, since Cush was related to Ham.

Her primary ministry was to model the godliness that God had ordained for those rightly related to Him by faith were to exhibit. But her faithfulness resulted in being privileged for a remarkable instance of prophetic ministry that proved to have global consequences in every generation for the next two thousand years.

I was also struck by her father's name, Phanuel. This name is adopted from the word used to describe the momentous occasion when Jacob wrestled with God and came face to face with the living Son of God. The word for "face to face" became the name of the place, Peniel. Here is a woman who lived in an intimate *viz a viz* relationship with the living God, constantly anticipating the fulfillment of His Word regarding the promised Savior. Small wonder then that the last prophetic word was delivered by one whose life of faith was known by the name of "Grace", (from which the name Anna derives).

Anna fell victim to widowhood early in life; but she wisely retreated into the bosom of the Heavenly Father. In the warmth of His eternal and unmerited love, she found it easy to devote her entire life, day and night, to worship, and to leading a remnant of people who shared her faith in the coming Messiah. Luke also suggests that when she was not leading others in praise and adoration, she counseled those who sought her out for a prophetic word concerning His will for their lives.

Since a prophet is one who reveals God's will in a situation, and speaks a word of counsel regarding its resolution, Anna was a true prophet. Yet, in this, her finest hour as a prophet, she becomes the mouthpiece of God to speak to the entire nation and world, thanks to the throng gathered about her as she speaks out so firmly and ecstatically, and, through the pen of Luke, to the entire world in every generation thereafter.

As the Savior is brought to be dedicated, fulfilling the Law, the moment becomes pregnant with prophetic meaning. Luke says that she left this incredible event to speak widely and forcefully to anyone who would listen, that the long awaited Messiah was now, physically, in their midst.

It is ironic that in this Temple, a male dominated ministry enterprise, God had selected not only a godly man, Simeon, to speak His Word, but reserved the last prophetic utterance for a female prophet. Anna delivered the final word from heaven about its true Son, to the last generation of the Old Testament. What an historic moment for females called to ministry by the Lord.

Summary

Now you know; from Eve to the final episode of the Old Testament, the presentation of Jesus in the Temple at Jerusalem, women were continually used by God to perform very important ministries.

Each appears at a very strategic moment. Each fulfills a strategic role of leadership that turns out to be crucial to the forward movement of redemptive history.

Of course, the men with whom they were allied do stand as among the leading figures of Old Testament era. Nevertheless, the record shows, in support of our contention, that in addition to the Patriarchs, God had also chosen Matriarchs to serve Him in ministry leadership.

Section 3: Female Ministry Leaders in the New Testament

The New Testament opens with the amazing story of a young virgin girl named Mary.

During her espousal to Joseph, the angel Gabriel visited Mary. The angel announced to Mary that she had "found favor with God" (Luke 1:30, NIV) and that she "will be with child and give birth to a son" whom she shall call Jesus (Luke 1:31, NIV).

Even though Mary could not fully grasp the significance of what she had just heard, or the effect that news would have on her impending marriage, her response to Gabriel was, "I am the Lord's servant. May it be to me as you have said" (Luke 1:38, NIV). Mary's faith, strength and her capacity to understand and deal with such strange, supernatural happenings and the related fallout were amazing.

Women in the Ministry of Jesus

During his public ministry, Jesus interacted with many women, including the woman of Samaria; Joanna; Susanna; Mary Magdalene; Mary and Martha; the woman with the alabaster box; the women found at his burial as well as those present at His resurrection, just to name a few.

It is fascinating to discover how Jesus treated those women, how He employed them in His service, and how they functioned with him in His public ministry. As an example of how He treated women, observe his encounter with the Samaritan woman at the well.

Think of the religious and cultural barriers that Jesus crossed in order to look for one woman – the woman of Samaria.[94] This woman had absolutely no status before a Jewish Rabbi because of three factors. First, she was a Samaritan, therefore every Jew considered her (and all Samaritans) untouchable. Second, she was a woman, and that meant that a man of the stature of Jesus could not even speak to her in public. Third, because of sin in her life, she was ostracized by her own village. But by speaking with her, Jesus marked her as a person of worth and value.

No wonder the disciples marveled (shocked) to see their Master in her company, seated, and conversing with her by the well. He then provoked her thinking toward His identity. Then, as He ministered to her, she found eternal life. She then confronted the village that had rejected and abused her with her transformation. As a result, the city of Samaria was evangelized.

Notice how she went about this task, with the blessing and favor of Jesus. She left her water pot and went into the city preaching Jesus and compelling the men, "come, see a man, which told me all things that ever I did: is not this the Christ?"[95] Her testimony caused many of the Samaritans to believe on Jesus and opened the door for the gospel to be preached in a two-day revival meeting led by Jesus himself. Imagine this: an early missionary event occurred because of the leadership of a woman.

Next, as you read the pages of the Gospel you discover that the compassion of Jesus for the lost drove Him to travel to many cities, proclaiming the good news of the kingdom of God.[96] In His ministering team were, of course, the disciples accompanying Him. Nevertheless, there were also women in the entourage.

Luke said, "The twelve were with Him, and also some women who had been cured of evil spirits and diseases: Mary (called Magdalene) from whom seven demons had come out; Joanna the wife of Cuza, the manager of Herod's household; Susanna; and many others."[97] The Bible tells us that these women were supporters of Jesus and His disciples "helping to support them out of their own means."[98]

However "Mary Magdalene, Joanna, Mary the mother of James, and the others with them"[99] were not just followers and supporters of the Lord in good times. During His apparent crises, including the final one, His crucifixion and burial, they were present. Even at His resurrection, who is it that breaks the news to the disciples but a woman. His first ministering witnesses were the women who ran to Peter and the others to tell them that He was not dead, but that He had risen from the dead and was very much alive.[100]

Mary Magdalene was the first to see the resurrected Christ and the first to preach the resurrection message.[101] She did not hesitate to proclaim the good news. She was not afraid of what men would say. She did not feel inferior. She did not choose to remain silent. She did not argue with Jesus that this was not a woman's role. Instead she quickly obeyed the Lord's command telling the good news that Jesus is not in the tomb, that death and the grave could not hold His body down, but that her Lord and Savior was alive forevermore.[102] She did the work of an evangelist because the Lord gave her the message and empowered her to tell it aboard. In this subtle act, Jesus made it clear that, to Him, women belonged in ministry.

During His earthly life, women ministered to and supported Jesus, including Mary and Martha. When Martha felt her sister was not sharing the workload in preparing a meal for Jesus and the Twelve, she confronted Him: "Lord, don't you care that my sister has left me to do the work by myself? Tell her to help me!" The Lord answered, "Martha, Martha, you are worried and upset about many things, but only one thing is needed. Mary has chosen what is better, and it will not be taken away from her."[103]

Leonard Swindler in *Biblical Affirmations of Women* said, "Luke's picture of Mary sitting at Jesus' feet in the posture of a disciple has been called perhaps the strongest and clearest affirmation on the part of Jesus that the intellectual and 'spiritual' life was just as proper to women as to men."[104]

One day Jesus sat at the dinner table in the house of one of the Pharisees, when a woman, "who had lived a sinful life in that town,"[105] showed up uninvited with an alabaster jar of very expensive perfume.

In a spirit of brokenness, she began to wash the feet of Jesus with her tears and dried them with her hair. She broke the bottle of precious ointment and poured the perfume on the feet of Jesus.

"When the Pharisee who had invited Him saw this, he said to himself, 'If this man was a prophet, he would know who was touching him and what kind of woman she is – that she is a sinner.' "[106] Whereas the Pharisee was quick in calling the woman a sinner, Jesus was quick in responding with love and compassion, even at the risk of His own reputation.

The disciples too, were very angry and sanctimoniously decried such a gesture wasteful, and the funds better used to deal with local poverty.

Jesus silenced such disingenuous criticism, describing her gesture as a noble work. He explained that she intended the gesture as a prophecy signaling His impending death by pre-anointing Him for burial. He then charged the disciples to recount this story in memory of her wherever the gospel is preached.[107]

Women Leaders Chosen by the Apostles

The Book of Acts records the descent of the Holy Spirit upon one hundred and twenty men and women who were waiting for the promise of the Father in the Upper Room.[108]

On the day of Pentecost, God confirmed that He is 'no respecter of persons' because, in one moment, and without hesitation, He empowered every single one of them through the infilling of the Holy Spirit. He even confirmed this Presence by giving them the ability to speak in unknown languages supernaturally, i.e., without ever having learned them and with such perfection that people hearing them concluded these people were speaking the language as their 'mother tongue'!

Notice that in this wonderful work of the Holy Spirit, we see that God had anointed both men and women for this initial prophetic ministry of preaching the Good News.

The Apostle Peter, who was the chief spokesperson, received a revelation from God concerning a prophecy recorded for the Jewish Bible from the Prophet Joel's prophetic Book that explained this phenomenon that had just come to pass:

> In the last days, God says, I will pour out my Spirit on all people. Your sons and daughters will prophesy, your young men will see visions, your old men will dream dreams. Even on my servants, BOTH MEN AND WOMEN, I will pour out my Spirit in those days, and they will prophesy.[109] (emphasis mine).

To prophesy is to declare the good news of the Kingdom. It is to preach the gospel. It is clear then from Scripture that God approves of women for this prophetic ministry as well as men.

The early church was blessed to have in its leadership many gifted women who helped the Apostle Paul, tremendously. We know this to be true because he mentions them by name in his Epistles often explaining that they held positions of authority.

Philip's Daughters

Aside from Paul, another disciple, Philip, the evangelist, had four daughters who engaged in active prophetic ministries.

Priscilla

Paul's writing also contains high praise of the many notable women who co-labored with him in the ministry. Of the thirty-nine co-workers mentioned in his letters, more than twenty-five percent were women. Priscilla and Aquila taught the eloquent Apollos, a mighty expounder of the Word, the Scriptures.[110] Priscilla and Aquila not only helped Paul as co-workers,[111] but were also pastors of a local church kept at their house in Corinth.[112] Paul held them in high esteem, as did members of all the gentile churches.[113]

Phoebe

One woman who came in for high commendation by Paul was Phoebe. Phoebe was a servant at the Church in Cenchrea.[114] The Greek word used here for servant is *diakonos*. Cunningham said, ". . . the word servant in Romans 16:1 describing Phoebe's office . . . is *diakonos* in the Greek. Almost everywhere in the New Testament, *diakonos* is translated as 'minister.' The word was used to describe a minister of the Gospel."[115] Phoebe is also spoken of as a succourer of many and of Paul.[116] The word *succourer* or *helper* in the Greek is *prostates*, which was used to describe exceptional leadership. The Jewish historian, Josephus, used this same word several times to describe Caesar.[117] Paul commanded the members of the church at Rome to receive her as such, and to help her in whatever manner she requested.

Junia

Paul also mentions that Andronicus and Junia were outstanding among the apostles (Romans 16:7), and there is little doubt that Junia was a feminine name. Actually, Junia(s) was in ministry before Paul; her ministry can be traced back to that of Jesus Christ.[118] She even spent time in prison for her prophetic ministry. Paul described her as an apostle. It is difficult to limit the authority, and scope of work, of an apostle. And such was our sister, Junia(s), a woman without limits in Christ, "outstanding among the apostles."[119] Both John Chrysostom and Jerome referred to her as a woman apostle, and no commentator referred to her as a man until the late thirteenth century.

Stephanas & Chloe

In 1 Corinthians 16:15 Paul urges the 'brothers' of the church to submit to Stephanas. Obviously, Stephanas, who was devoted to serving the saints, must have been a woman in authority for Paul to require submission of the men! Chloe could have been a leader of a house church.[120]

Eunice and Lois

Paul recognized Eunice and Lois as the ones responsible for nurturing and teaching young Timothy in the faith.[121] He also, in his writings made mention of these women:

Euodia(s), Syntyche, Mary, Persis, Tryphena and Tryphosa were all women who co-labored with Paul to do the work of the ministry.

So much evidence written into the Word of God that Jesus has indeed called and anointed women to every area of work in the church.

Lydia and Other Women

Another associate of Paul's, Lydia, a seller of purple dye, opened her home for ministry (Acts 16:40), as did many other Christian women in the Roman Empire, including the "elect lady" to whom John addressed his second epistle. Close examination of 2 John would suggest that she was functioning in a pastoral capacity, as would also have been the case for Lydia (Acts 16:40), Nympha (Colossians 4:15), and Chloe (I Corinthians 1:11).

Summary

The women of the New Testament did not come behind in any area of ministry. They were as much a significant part of the establishment and expansion of the program of God, as were those women of the Old Testament.

Where would the church be without the holiness, faith, courage and maturity of Mary, the mother of Jesus? Where would the Samaritans of Jesus' day be without the timely evangelism of the woman at the well? Joanna, Susanna, Mary Magdalene and the other women did not stop short of following Jesus wherever he went.

These women not only supported his ministry from their own means, but when the disciples lost faith in Jesus, those women followed to the bitter end of his death and burial, and were there at His glorious resurrection, being the first ones to receive and carry the resurrection message. Mary, the sister of Martha, chose to be discipled by Jesus, a role the Lord described as the "one thing . . . needed" and "will not be taken away from her."[122] The woman with the alabaster jar of very expensive perfume survived the scorn of the Pharisees and the criticism of the disciples when, despite their uproar, she broke the jar of perfume and lavished it upon the feet of Jesus in preparation for his burial.

The apostles too, followed in the footsteps of the Lord so far as the participation of women in the work of the church is concerned. Peter, full of the Holy Ghost on the Day of Pentecost, confirmed the public ministry of the women by reiterating Joel's prophecy: "your . . . daughters will prophesy."[123]

The apostle Paul, who appears to be demanding silence from church women, has shown otherwise by acknowledging the prominent positions women enjoyed in the New Testament church, including Priscilla, Phoebe, and Junia, to name a few.

The Bible bears clear witness that as far as Jesus and the Apostles were concerned, women belong in leadership.

ENDNOTES

87 Alvera Mickelsen, "An Egalitarian View: There is Neither Male nor Female in Christ," in Women in Ministry: Four Views, ed. Bonnidell Clouse and Robert G. Clouse (Downers Grove, Ill.: Intervarsity Press, 1989), 171-206.

88 Aida Dina Spencer, *Beyond the Curse: Women Called to Ministry* (Nashville: Thomas Nelson, 1985), 21. Quoted in Cunningham & Hamilton, 251.

89 Vine. , 208.

90 Mickelsen, 183.

91 Frances Brown, S.R. Driver, Charles A. Briggs, A Hebrew and English Lexicon of the Old Testament (Boston: Houghton Mifflin, 1907), 617.

92 David Freedman, "Woman, a Power Equal to Man," Biblical Archaeology Review , January/February 1983, pp. 56-58. Quoted in Mickelsen, 183.

93 Gen. 1:31.

94 Jn. 4.

95 Jn. 4:29 (KJV).

96 Lk. 8:1.

97 Lk. 8:1-3 (NIV).

98 Lk. 8:3 (NIV).

99 Lk. 24:9-10 (NIV).

100 Mt 28:8-10.

101 Mk 16:9-10.

102 Jn. 20:17-18.

103 Lk. 10:38-41.

104 Leonard Swindler, Biblical Affirmations of Women (Philadelphia: Westminster, 1979), 192. Quoted in Tucker & Liefeld, 26.

105 Lk. 7:37 (NIV).

106 Lk. 7:39 (NIV).

107 Mt 26:6-13.

108 Ac 1:13, 15; 2:1-4.

109 Ac 2:17-18 (NIV).

110 Ac 18:24-26.

111 Ro 16:3.

112 1 Co 16:19.

113 Ro 16:3-4.

114 Ro 16:1.

115 Cunningham & Hamilton, 53.

116 Ro 16:2.

117 Cunningham & Hamilton, 54.

118 Ro 16:7.

119 Ibid.

120 1 Co 1:11.

121 2 Ti 1:5.

122 Lk. 10:41(NIV).

123 Ac 2:17 (NIV).

Chapter 9

Church Mothers

Introduction

When we think of Church History, we think of the volumes written about the "Church Fathers", those theological and pastoral leaders God used so mightily in the centuries after the death of the Apostles.

To a man, they embraced the "Socratic bias" regarding the nature and function of women as inferior. In this, they resembled their rabbinic predecessors, who railed against women participating in Jewish worship except as a backbench observer.

Yet, as such rabbinic prejudice failed to impress God that women did not belong in leadership; neither did He exclude women fulfilling important roles.

Church historians, Ruth A. Tucker & Walter L. Liefeld wrote a book, *Daughters of the Church: Women and Ministry from New Testament Times to the Present,* detailing the role of women in church leadership.

They wrote, "Although the medieval world was greatly influenced by women, there was a strong underlying current that "envisaged women as inferior—endowed with less spiritual insight than men and incapable of the highest forms of Christian ministry."[124]

To appreciate the truthfulness of the insights of these writers, consider these quotes:

- Tertullian (AD 160 -230): "Do you not know that you are each an Eve? The sentence of God on this sex of yours lives in this age: the guilt must of necessity live too. You are the Devil's gateway: You are the unsealer of the forbidden tree: You are the first deserter of the divine law: You are she who persuaded him whom the devil was not valiant enough to attack. You destroyed so easily God's image, man. On account of your desert even the Son of God had to die."[125]

- St Augustine of Hippo: "What is the difference whether it is in a wife or a mother, it is still Eve the temptress that we must beware of in any woman...I fail to see what use woman can be to man, if one excludes the function of bearing children. ". . . only the man possesses the full image of God."[126]

- Chrysostom (AD 345-407): "A woman is the second authority" that should not "demand equality, for she is under the head."[127] In his opinion, while the man is "skilled at the greater things" he is "downright inept and useless in the performance of the less important ones, so that the woman's service is necessary" and that God has "assigned . . . the less important, inferior matters to the woman." [128]

Yet, these comments neither reflect the thinking of every church Father, nor do they sum up the thinking of these writers. Often, one can find their writings conveying ideas about women that contradict these statements.

Sometimes the Church Fathers frowned on church women and at other times, they applauded them. According to Tucker and Liefeld, "women were sometimes thought to be deceived, lascivious, and incapable, but they were also lauded as mothers, martyrs, intelligent students and teachers of Scripture, and – as some men acknowledged – as cherished friends."[129]

From these discrepancies, we can conclude that the influence of Socratic thinking about women created a conflict between theology and experience. The failure of the Church Fathers "to reach any consistent viewpoint"[130] is evidenced in a quotation by Elizabeth Clark:

> The most fitting word with which to describe the Church Fathers' attitude toward women is ambivalence. Women were God's creation, his good gift to men – and the curse of the world. They were weak in both mind and character – and displayed dauntless courage, undertook prodigious feats of scholarship. Vain, deceitful, brimming with lust – they led men to Christ, fled sexual encounter, wavered not at the executioner's threat, adorned themselves with sackcloth and ashes.[131]

In support of this assessment, I offer these examples of the ambivalent thinking of the Church Fathers regarding women.

John Chrysostom

John Chrysostom "in his homily on 1 Timothy . . . states that Paul 'wishes the man to be preeminent in every way.' Eve 'taught the man once, upset everything, and made him liable to disobedience'. . ."[132] Commenting on Paul's statement, 'I do not permit a woman to teach,' Chrysostom "compares one's going to a woman for instruction to his going to the 'irrational animals of the lower kind' like the ant of Proverbs 6:6."[133]

Yet this same man celebrated the outstanding women whom Paul mentioned in Romans 16. Regarding Mary, whose hard work Paul commended in verse 6, he said, "Christians are both honored and shamed by having her among us . . . in that we men are left so far behind by such women." He also wrote glowingly of Junia (whom he understood to be a woman), who's devotion made her worthy to be called an apostle.[134]

Thomas Aquinas

Thirteenth century theologian, Thomas Aquinas, described women as "defective and accidental . . . a male gone awry . . . probably . . . the result of some weakness in the father's generative power . . . ."[135] Aquinas argued, "women were unsuited for any meaningful role in the church or society."[136]

Yet "his case against the ordination of women included arguments in their favor."[137] He said, "Women had been prophets, (he viewed the prophetic office as higher than that of priest), that women could possess some 'perfection' even as men, and that ordination pertained to the soul and the soul has no sex."[138]

While theologians of the patristic and medieval periods of church history struggled with their theology versus their experience concerning women, leaders of the Renaissance movement, the secular counterpart to the Reformation, openly challenged the thinking of the church regarding the role and inferiority of women. Erasmus, for instance, "had a much higher view of women than did medieval theologians."[139] Agrippa of Nettesheim, too, "argued that women in no way are inherently inferior to men" and "in some respects superior to men."[140]

Therefore, as we examine the roles of women throughout church history we are face to face with the perennial conflict between how the male leadership of the church viewed women, and how God viewed and used them. Against the assertions typical of those mentioned above, we find God calling women to leadership roles and using them in ways that often determined the future of His work in their midst!

Map of Chapter

We shall look at many women's lives in this chapter. To guide you as to the timeline of when these women lived and served, we shall divide this chapter into three sections.

In Section One, we will look at outstanding women from the era that begins with the first post-apostolic generation, and ends with the Reformation.

In Section Two, you will meet fascinating women to whom the Reformers turned for leadership.

In Section Three, we will examine some outstanding female leaders who served the Lord from the close of the Reformation through the modern era.

Section One: Church Mothers (Centuries 2 through 15)

As Christianity spread during the early post-apostolic era, women continued to fulfill vital roles as leaders. Their blood joined their male counterparts in the arenas, stakes, and upon crosses.

Here we will recount some of the many who heroically helped build the church with their lives, gifts, and blood.

Third Century

Catherine of Alexandria
This brave woman defended the faith at Alexandria before philosophers and courtiers. As a result Maxentius, son of Roman Emperor, Maximian, had her tortured to death.

Dorothy of Caesarea
A contemporary of Catherine of Alexandria, Dorothy was martyred in A.D. 313. During her walk to her execution, a lawyer named Theophilus taunting her, requested that she give him a basket of flowers and fruit. As she was readied for death, a small girl came up to her to give her a basket of flowers and fruit. She directed the girl to deliver it to Theophilus. He was so touched by the incident that he became a believer, and was subsequently martyred.

Macrina the Younger
This brave woman pioneered in the development of the monastic life, founding a religious community for women in Eastern Europe. She healed, prophesied, and actively spread the faith. John Chrysostom wrote of her, "she was a great organizer, and independent thinker, and as well educated." After the death of her mother, she reared and educated her younger brother Peter, who became Bishop of Sebaste.

Marcella
At her palace, Marcella became an important voice to interact with heretics and bring them to a clear understanding of the Christian truth. She held an

important teaching post. Jerome, the renowned Church Father who made the first translation of the Bible, was so impressed with her ability to teach the Word that when a dispute arose in Rome concerning the meaning of the Scriptures, Jerome asked her to settle it. She promoted the idea of Church in the Home, and built a model that was widely replicated to plant churches. She also organized Bible studies and prayer fellowships, and led projects to benefit the poor and needy. She later established a religious retreat for women at the edge of the city of Rome. Her ministry spawned important projects led by two of her female disciples. She also built a rudimentary seminary on the outskirts of the city and established the first hospitals in Rome.

Paula

Marcella introduced one of her trained disciples, a female leader named Paula to Jerome. He chose Paula to assist him in making the Latin translation of the Scriptures. Imagine that! The first translation involved a brilliant Hebrew, Greek, and Latin scholar and a FEMALE associate who managed revision chores and even handled some of the work of preparing a Latin translation from the Hebrew and Greek texts. In turn, Jerome dedicated some of his books to her. Paula founded three convents and a monastery in Bethlehem where they copied and distributed Biblical manuscripts. Their model for preparing and spreading the written Bible was replicated in monasteries for many centuries.

Fourth Century

Genieve

When Attila and his Huns invaded France in 451 a woman named Genieve rose to leadership. Because of her ministry, Paris was spared from destruction on two important occasions.

The first incident was to lead a prayer movement. As the Huns marched toward France, she assured the inhabitants of Paris that God would protect them if they would pray. While the men prepared for battle, she persuaded the women to pray for hours in the church. After having destroyed Orleans, Attila turned his troops in another direction, thereby leaving Paris untouched. The second miraculous incident occurred when a famine struck Paris, Genieve organized a band of prayer warriors who interceded for Paris, averting a famine by miraculously finding ingredients, and baking and distributing free bread.

Bridget

In Ireland, one woman became a leading ministry figure, Bridget. After settling in the region of Kildare, she established a house for refuge, devotion and worship. It became the model for similar house ministries throughout Ireland.

Fifth Century

Bishop Theodora

Justinian, one of the Christian Emperors who succeeded Constantine, was, for all practical purposes, head of the Church of his generation. His wife, Theodora, became an outstanding leader throughout Rome. A mosaic plaque in a church in the city of Rome commemorates her leadership; the inscription reads, "Theodora Episcopa" or "Theodora, the Bishop". The word bishop is in the feminine case, proving that it meant that a lady was serving in the capacity of a bishop.

Sixth Century

Hilda the Theological Professor

Midway into this century, a seminary for men and women was founded in the British Isles. A woman named Hilda was appointed as a leader on the faculty in the field of theology. Several of her students and disciples became leading church theologians and pastors, and one, a man named Caedmon, became the earliest known poet in England.

Tenth Century

Brunhilda the Writer

In Germany and central Europe, a noted theologian became a renowned writer. She also spoke out to confront the sins of leading male spiritual leaders of her day, both in the church and in the world of politics. She was able to influence some of the outstanding leaders including Frederick Bararossa, as well as other kings, and leading ministry figures. She performed many miracles during her long ministry career.

Twelfth Century

Clare

Now we come to the time when the outstanding minister, Francis of Assisi, preached the Gospel. However few know that he shared his ministry with a partner, whose name was Clare. She built many ministry centers throughout Italy, France, Spain and Germany. Near the end of her life, while lame, her congregation was attacked by the Saracens. She insisted that her associates carry her to the front door where she personally confronted these Muslim warriors, then prayed in a loud voice for God to deliver the defenseless believers under her care. She then experienced the presence of the Lord saying, "I do have these people in My care". She then turned to the people and said, "Do not fear anyone!" The Saracens fled, considering her words 'magical'.

Thirteenth through Fifteenth Centuries

We can only mention their names but many of these women remain familiar to Christians today. These outstanding female leaders included:

- Hechthild of Magdeburg
- Gertrude the Great
- Angela of Foligno
- Bridget of Sweden
- Catherine of Sienna
- Catherine of Sweden
- Margery Kempe
- Joan of Arc
- Isabella of Castile, and
- Maragaret Beaufort.

Imagine the spiritual poverty that would have resulted if these women had not been called by God to ministry leadership!

Section Two: Women of the Reformation Era (Centuries 15 through 17)

From the beginnings of Christianity, women have preached. In the Reformation, they began to shine as pulpiteers.

One thinks of the sisters, converted to Christ under the preaching of St. Francis of Assisi, who became his students. Thanks to his diligent discipleship, their theological knowledge surpassed that of the theological scholars who visited from Rome. Francis used them to fill the daily pulpit that attracted audiences of thousands.

Hildegard of Bingen

Then there is the incredible theological scholar and preacher, Hildegard of Bingen. This medieval woman, in the 12th century was granted ecclesiastical permission to preach publicly on particular occasions. That permission was based, however, on the conviction that she was an exceptional woman who had been granted special gifts and graces by God.

In the 15th and 16th centuries, the Body of Christ started to challenge the theological assumption that Scripture requires women's subordination and silence in the church. In the pre-Reformation era, women in the Lollard movement had preached and read the Bible in the worship service.

Their early prominence was due to a core tenet of Reformation theology—the priesthood of all believers. This explains how women served so prominently in vocational ministry prior to the time when it fell firmly into the hands of those male leaders we all associate with being Reformers.

Nevertheless, in the early phase of the Reformation, liberated women occupied roles of ministry leadership. Then the Socratic cloud of male superiority began to cast its shadow; female roles were once again subjugated to men and opportunities for pulpit ministry officially eliminated. However, prior to this clampdown, there are some remarkable stories of women preachers. I have chosen three to illustrate this point.

Argula von Grumback (1492- 1563)

During the Reformation, a member of the Bavarian nobility, Argula von Grumback, challenged the Rector and the entire faculty of the University of Ingolstadt to a debate in which she would defend the principles of the Protestant Reformation. She offered to base this debate upon a translation of the Bible published prior to the outbreak of the Reformation. She was permitted to present her position in 1523 in Nuremberg before the heads of the Empire.

Martin Luther describes her as, "that most noble woman, *Argula von Stauffer,* is there making a valiant fight with great spirit, boldness of speech and knowledge of Christ." Her extensive education and fine critical abilities enabled her to become a force to be reckoned with. She conducted church meetings in her home and officiated at funerals.

Margaret of Navarre and Jeanne d'Albret

Two other important leaders of the Protestant Reformation during this period were Margaret of Navarre (1492-1549) and her daughter, Jeanne d'Albret (1528-1572). Margaret became the grandmother of King Henry IV of France. He issued the Edict of Nantes, granting religious toleration to the French Protestants for almost a century. Jeanne d'Albret held services of the new Reformed faith in her palace apartment. A friend of John Calvin, she also used her palace as an institute for Reformation study.

Marie Dentière of Geneva

Marie Dentière of Geneva came to public attention through a Reformation Day sermon preached by a woman, Isabelle Graesslé, who made reference to her. A very influential preacher, her success attracted another woman to the calling of preacher, Madame Claude. Think about it; in the years prior to Calvin's arrival in Geneva, these women prominently preached each Sunday. Only after Calvin was firmly established in the city, were they forced to return to the role of "keeping silent" in the church.

Yes, the dark cloud of Socratic thinking finally hovered over the Reformation Movement, greatly retarding the church's growth by restricting women from ministry leadership.

Fortunately, it could not prevent the Holy Spirit from choosing and using the gifts of women for ministry leadership. As a result, this Movement is credited with ushering in the dawn of a new day for women in clergy vocations, especially among those in the segment of the Reformation involving "non-conformist" groups that dominated the mid-seventeenth century, also called the "Civil War Sects".

Women in the English Non-Conformity (Protestant) Movement

Studies of this period portray female preachers as respected sober minded people who displayed a distinctive sense of calling; and who were largely, embraced by the true Believing community. (Some of these women we will shortly examine more closely).

It is remarkable that such a record even exists, since contemporary church historians tended to either ignore or downplay the contribution of women preachers to the advancement of the kingdom. A list of religious radical leaders published in that period includes about 1000 names, but only 40 of women. Yet records of churches posting membership roles reflect, on average, a 50% female population. So how did women gain the level of acceptance to move into preaching ministries? There were five avenues that led to women being accepted for ministry leadership.

First Avenue: Persecution

Ironically, persecution was the one area in which women were welcome to participate. Women bore their fair share of torture and abuse. For example, in one congregation where 19 people received punishment for "crimes", 12 were women. In time, suffering earned female leaders the respect of the male leaders. Eventually, for those who survived prison and torture, the Body of Christ welcomed them to pulpit ministries.

Second Avenue: Children's Ministry

One area where women dominated was in the discipleship and instruction of children in the home. As a result, the widespread ministry experienced an unintended consequence. When the children grew to adulthood, they were comfortable with female leadership since they had grown up under their tutelage. Hence, the instruction of children became the path to the acceptance of women in the pulpit.

Third Avenue: Hospitality Ministry

Women also developed another avenue to leadership. In the beginning, they played vital roles by making their homes centers of hospitality for the local congregation. This led to many of their homes being used for public worship and this, in turn, became the springboard for women assuming the pulpit responsibilities, and produced many of the important tracts used to evangelize the lost. Again, this ministry had its unintended consequence. Women became the church planters, using homes and rented halls.

One woman, Mrs. Dorothy Hazzard, seceded from her husband's parish in 1640, with four men, to establish the Separatist Congregation later known as Broadmead Bristol. Meeting at first in her own home, the congregation quickly grew to almost 163 members.

A small group of women, along with a few men, founded the church that called John Bunyan as pastor.

Fourth Avenue: Fund-raisers

Women were instrumental in securing financial support for a pastor of a budding church plant. They would arrange for a wealthy woman associated with their ministry to hire the man as her family's "Chaplain". This is how Sussex College of Cambridge University was founded. As was true in Jesus and the Apostle Paul's ministry, women were substantial financial supporters.

Fifth Avenue: Tract Publication

Women also contributed much to the Reformation ministry related to getting out the Word through Tracts, Sermons and other printed materials. Think about it: since women wrote and published so many sermons, don't you suppose these were being preached somewhere by them? Among these leaders, Sara Jones comes to mind. In 1632, she was jailed for her outspoken religious convictions. While incarcerated, she penned several sermons and tracts. Another woman who enjoyed wide acclaim as a preacher in print was Catherine Chidley. She wrote one of the most widely read books, *The Justification of the Independent Churches of Christ.*

The Reformation Movement inherited the thinking of the Lollard movement regarding allowing women to preach in pulpits (who readily granted women licenses to preach the Word). So as late as the 1590's, church historians report that women were preaching in Reformation pulpits. However, as the Movement matured, women were told to sit down and shut up, except under certain conditions. Women could preach if:

- The evidence that their gifts were so extraordinary that the sign of their call to preach was undeniable; and,
- Men were not available to fill such pulpits where audiences were made up largely of infidels.

This view was also that of such Reformation leaders as John Calvin, Peter Martyr, and the Dutch Calvinist, Gisbertus Voetius.

Among Reformers in the Netherlands, women were permitted to preach in the congregations of the Baptists. Later, these same groups allowed women to preach in Baptist churches in New England.

In any large metropolitan area, the process by which women gained access to pulpits generally followed the path of a large group of Baptists in London.

At first, this London church allowed women to assemble for their own spiritual meetings. Out of these meetings, women with gifts and skills began to deliver public sermons to general audiences on subjects relative to female issues. These meetings grew to audiences of thousands.

As a result, by mid seventeenth century, in London, several women preached in pulpits. Yet throughout the period, the controversy as to the legitimacy of gender ministry issues persisted. While the practice did not gain general approval, still, historians suspect that more women preached than the records show.

In summary, does not the record of church history confirm that women contributed substantially to the growth of almost all segments of the Reformation Movement, especially in the segments known as the Puritan and Separatist movements? Women, through the various avenues described here, gained the respect of male leaders, who trusted them with pulpit responsibilities. Truly, this was the work of the Holy Spirit, since it stands in stark contrast to the view of women held by the popular culture of that day.

The non-church (secular) culture was marked by a deep disparity between the place of men and women. One of their leading enlightened authors, James Boswell, expressed his fear that the inequality of women would continue even in heaven.

Nevertheless, change did happen; and it would be led by the Quaker movement. This became the only one group that genuinely appointed women to pulpit ministries. They even wrote it into their Doctrinal Statements and By-Laws. We shall deal with this in the next Part.

Quakers and the Emergence of Women Preachers

The early history of attitudes towards gender in the Religious Society of Friends (aka Quakers) is particularly notable for providing for one of the largest and most equitable roles for women in the Christian tradition at the time, despite not endorsing universal equality until much later. Quaker views regarding women in ministry have always been considered progressive in their own time (beginning in the 17th century), and in the late 19th century this tendency bore fruit in the prominence of Quaker women in the American women's rights movement.

For many outside observers during the first hundred years of Quakerism, the most surprising aspect of Quakerism was the fact that "ministry" – the prerogative to speak during a Quaker meeting – was open to women from the very beginnings of the movement in the 1650s.

In James Boswell's *Life of Johnson,* Samuel Johnson's opinion of a female Quaker preacher was recorded thus: "sir, a woman's preaching is like a dog's walking on his hind legs. It is not done well; but you are surprised to find it done at all." Especially in the early years, a large number — even possibly the majority – of traveling Quaker preachers were women. Aside from ministry, Quaker women were allowed to travel alone and publish, which was also unusual for the time.

For many Quakers, both historical and contemporary, the inclusion of women is part of the "Testimony of Equality."

However, despite that testimony, women's roles were not equal for many years. Meetings for Business were segregated by sex, with separate meetings for women and men responsible for different things; this separation was eased during the 19th century and eliminated later.

Nevertheless, allowing women to exercise authority over any business at all – let alone authority over men (in the form of approving or denying marriages) – was a radical move in the 17th century. It provided women the opportunity to run organizations. That acquired experience enabled women to, later on, lead the Women's Suffrage and Abolition movements.

Elizabeth Hooten

Elizabeth Hooten was the first convert of George Fox, when he was 22 years of age, and the first woman to become a Quaker preacher. She was close to fifty years old at the time. Fox's words met a need in her. She was frustrated with the "dead" and compromising Baptist assembly she attended.

Soon afterward, Elizabeth felt a "call" from God to preach. She left her family and began to urge judgment and repentance across England. Because of her outspokenness, she soon found herself in prison. Indeed, she went to prison many times in her life. Other abuse followed her, too.

In Boston authorities took her for a two-day walk into the Massachusetts forest and abandoned her there to starve. Although over sixty at the time, she survived, finding her way to Rhode Island.

In England, some cattle she owned were confiscated. She petitioned Charles II of England, and used the opportunity to share the Gospel with him. To get rid of her, the king gave her a letter saying she might settle anywhere she liked in Britain's American colonies. New England's authorities scorned the paper.

In Lincoln, she landed a three-month jail sentence for disturbing a congregation at worship. Quakers felt that most of what passed as worship was a facade. To warn souls, Elizabeth sometimes even donned sackcloth and ashes, and interrupted services, admonishing shocked audiences.

Elizabeth Hooten is an important link in the movement of women preachers from England to the Colonies.

Women Helping Lead the Reformation in the New World

To acquaint you, dear reader, with some of the female ministry leaders who made the greatest contributions, permit me to share four examples.

Anne Hutchinson (1591-1643)

During the Puritan era, Anne Hutchinson became influential in Boston, and opened her home to large classes of women. It is estimated that as many as eighty overflowed to the doorsteps of her house, at a time when Boston had a population of roughly 1,000 people.

These meetings grew rapidly, and soon men also attended, including Henry Vane, who served for a short time as governor of the Massachusetts Bay Colony. Within two years of her arrival from England, she had the strongest following of any leader in the entire colony. Her large following, coupled with her strong exegetical and preaching skills and Biblical knowledge created jealousy among New England ministers. They accused her of heresy and banished her from the Massachusetts Bay Colony in 1638.

Margaret Fell (1614-1702)

Many consider this woman to be the mother of Quakerism. She was an English peeress and wife of Judge Thomas Fell, member of the Long Parliament and Vice-Chancellor of Lancaster. Her home became a place of refuge and renewal for the persecuted Quakers for almost fifty years. Eventually, she was arrested and sentenced to four years for holding Quaker meetings in her home. After her release from prison, she visited Quakers in jails and traveled on horseback with her daughters and servants to remote farms and villages as an itinerant preacher. Many people sought wisdom and advice from her, including George Fox, who married her a number of years after the death of her husband. Because she had his blessing in her preaching ministry, she wrote many tracts and letters on the subject of women in ministry.

Madame Guyon (1648-1717)

This sainted French woman was imprisoned on several occasions for long periods because of her beliefs, but she never complained. She wrote forty books, including a twenty-volume commentary of the Bible. She had a wide following, particularly in France and Switzerland. Among those profoundly influenced by her ministry was Archbishop Francois Fenelon.

***Barbara Heck* (1734-1804)**

Barbara Heck was the founder of the first Methodist congregation in America. Think of her contribution to cement congregations that took the fruit of the Wesley revival and planted it into congregations where the new believers could grow, and the movement flourish for Christ. How did this woman arrive in America? She was sent there by Lady Selina Hastings, Countess of Huntingdon, and founder of the Calvinistic Methodist denomination during the Evangelical Awakening.

This woman functioned as a bishop by virtue of her right as a peeress to appoint Anglican clergymen as household chaplains and assign their duties, and to purchase presentation rights to chapels, enabling her to decide who would conduct services and preach. Among the many chaplains whom she appointed and continued to finance for many decades was George Whitefield. Then, would you believe, in 1779, after sixty chapels were already functioning under her auspices, this practice was disallowed by a consistory court of London. Fortunately, thanks to some clever thinking, her ministry was able to continue, under the newly passed Toleration Act, by registering her chapels as dissenting places of worship, known as "The Countess of Huntingdon's Connexion."

This movement was supported by another able female ministry leader known as Lady Selina.

Lady Selina

This gallant woman frequently invited members of the aristocracy to her home to hear the preaching of the Wesleys, Whitefield, Isaac Watts, Philip Doddridge, Benjamin Ingham, John Fletcher, John Berridge, William Romaine, Henry Venn, and others. She founded Trevecca House on property adjoining the home of Howel Harris. A seminary for the training of ministers for all denominations, its first president was John Fletcher. Joseph Benson eventually became headmaster on John Wesley's recommendation. George Whitefield preached the inaugural sermon when it opened in 1768.

Therefore, now that we understand the roots of the first female led Methodist congregation in the New World, we are ready to understand the role of women preachers in the two centuries that spanned the post-Reformation era to the twentieth century.

Section Three: Women Preachers of the Modern Era (Centuries 19 and 20)

The modern era began with a marvelous outpouring of the Holy Spirit upon the New World that also touched English speaking regions of Europe, known as the Second Great Awakening. We shall look at outstanding female ministry leaders in the evangelical movement and then those that dominated the rise of the Pentecostal and Holiness movements.

Female Leaders of the Evangelical Movement

In its formative period, several women preachers contributed to the Second Great Awakening (1800-1808): Deborah Pierce of New York; Martha Howell of Utica, New York; Phoebe Palmer, Catherine Booth, and Hannah Whitehall Smith.

Phoebe Palmer

Known as, "The Mother of the Holiness Movement", Phoebe Palmer began her ministry in 1835 with her Tuesday Meetings for the Promotion of Holiness. These continued for 39 years in New York City where she lived with her husband, a physician.

Her ministry profoundly affected hundreds of Methodist preachers, including at least five bishops. Her success encouraged other women to conduct the same type of ministry, and dozens of them sprang up throughout North America. These meetings brought together Christians of many denominations under the leadership of women, particularly among Methodists, Congregationalists, Episcopalians, Baptists, and Quakers.

In 1867, her husband purchased the periodical *GUIDE TO HOLINESS*. Under her able editorship, circulation grew from 13,000 to

30,000 subscribers. She traveled widely with her husband, conducting evangelistic meetings during the summer months.

The next summer, in Hamilton, Ontario, they attracted crowds of several thousand people. Suddenly, an afternoon prayer meeting became a ten-day revival meeting with four hundred conversions. This experience led to similar successes in New York City and in England that lasted four years where she preached to packed houses. *Phoebe Palmer* brought over 25,000 people to faith in Christ during her lifetime.

Catherine Booth (1829-1890)

Catherine Booth, with her husband, William Booth, founded the Christian Revival Association in 1865 and the Salvation Army in 1878. The Booths regarded the active participation of women to be vital to Christianity. Before 1865, when they were still Methodists, Catherine began preaching. Soon after her pulpit debut, her husband became ill, and his slow recovery paved the way for her own preaching ministry. She eventually became one of the most famous female preachers of England, and her last sermon was delivered to an audience of 50,000 people.

Evangeline Booth

I would be remiss if I failed to include the youngest daughter of William and Catherine Booth (founders of the Salvation Army) since she became the leading light after their retirement. This vivacious, attractive woman began preaching when only fifteen. In a few years, she was given her own ministry leadership in London.

Locals began calling her, "White Angel of the Slums." Her inventive approach to ministry led her to don the same tattered clothes as the flower girls in order to minister to them. She also developed the skill of problem solving to the point that her father, General William Booth, would send her into locations where the Army was in strife and disarray.

Eventually, she was appointed leader of the American work and became an American citizen. And later, in 1934, she became General of the worldwide movement, a position she held for five years.

In her travels, Evangeline's powerful lectures were published in a book titled *Toward a Better World.* She also wrote many hymns.

Hannah Whitehall Smith

This woman preacher was the author of *The Christian's Secret of a Happy Life (1875).* She catalyzed the development of the Holiness movement in Britain and throughout Europe. Her activities in England led to the Keswick Convention in 1874 which became a network of spacious summer vacation Bible Conference Centers in the US, Canada, and Britain hosting preachers who spoke about the deeper life.

Gladys Aylward

Finally, we can not ignore the contribution of women to pioneer missions. For this, we shall look at the extraordinary ministry of Gladys Aylward, and her work in China.

As a young teenager, Gladys read an article about the need for missionaries in China and it transformed her life. The idea that there existed millions of people in that distant land who had not yet heard of God's love moved her to go tell them the Good News. She attended missionary training school. But after the first quarter, mission authorities disqualified her from serving in China.

Aylward got a job as a housemaid. She saved until she could purchase a ticket on a train that made the long trek across Europe and Russia, which was at war with China and Japan. She almost lost her life several times crossing war zones. She was also briefly arrested in Russia. Finally, she arrived in Yangchen, China, where she took up work assisting a retired missionary lady at an inn for muleteers.

Aylward learned the Chinese language, a feat she called "one of God's great miracles." (The mission agency based their disqualification on her inability to learn that language).

Sharing the Gospel in the surrounding villages, she began to care for wounded soldiers and take in unwanted children. Before long, she had 60 to care for, that eventually grew to a hundred.

The Japanese put out a bounty for her capture—dead or alive. This forced her to leave her beloved "Inn of Sixth Happiness" amid a hale of bullets to lead 100 orphans on foot for one hundred miles over the mountains. After 27 exhausting days and shivering nights, she brought her children safely into Sian and collapsed. When the examining physicians learned that this woman had made this walk while suffering from typhus, pneumonia, relapsing fever, malnutrition, and supreme exhaustion they could not believe she made it.

Once she regained her strength, she resumed her ministry in this new region, sharing the Gospel in the villages, prisons and among lepers. Throughout her years in China, her ministry was characterized by a humble dependence upon God in a steady stream of extreme circumstances.

Gladys Aylward is a classic example of a female leader, being rejected by male leadership for ministry, and then proving them wrong by the blessing and leading of God.

Now we shall meet some of the women who helped lead the development of the Pentecostal movement.

Female Leaders of the Pentecostal Movement

You are about to meet some giants among those who helped light the fires of revival in the Pentecostal movement.

Carrie Judd Montgomery

Carrie Judd Montgomery was a healing evangelist of considerable prominence beginning in 1879, and became a founding member, along with A. B. Simpson, of the Christian and Missionary Alliance in 1887. She later became a part of the Pentecostal revival and was ordained a minister by the Assemblies of God in 1917, continuing in ministry until 1946.

Maria B. Woodworth-Etter

This capable woman became involved in the Holiness movement before she rose to prominence as an early Pentecostal leader. In 1884, she was licensed to preach by the Churches of God general conference, founded by John Winebrenner in 1825. Within a few months of this time, her meetings were already beginning to receive national press coverage, and in the late 1880s, she started twelve churches, added 1,000 members, erected six church buildings, and started several Sunday Schools. Her work at this time resulted in the licensing of twelve preachers. The revivals that she held at this time were accompanied with unusual manifestations of God's power, many healings, and mass conversions. During the early Pentecostal movement, Woodworth-Etter was in continual demand, becoming a featured speaker at the Worldwide Pentecostal Camp Meeting at Arroyo Seco, California, in April 1913. She founded the Woodworth-

Etter's Tabernacle in western Indianapolis in 1918, which she pastored until her death in 1924.

Other Pentecostal Female Leaders

Among Maria Woodworth-Etter's contemporaries, we should at least mention Florence L. Crawford, Mabel Smith, Ivey Campbell, and Rachel A. Sizelov. In the first decade of the twentieth century, these were some of the first women to spread the blessings of the early Pentecostal revival through their separate itinerant ministries. Florence Crawford planted and pastored several churches in the Pacific Northwest, founding and becoming general overseer of the Apostolic Faith Church based in Portland, Oregon, which later became part of the Open Bible Standard Denomination.

Other pioneers of the Pentecostal movement in the U.S. include:

- Mrs. Scott Ladd, who opened a Pentecostal mission in Des Moines in 1907
- The Duncan sisters, who had opened the Rochester Bible Training School at Elim Faith Home
- "Mother" Barnes of St. Louis, Missouri, who, with her son-in-law, B. F. Lawrence, held tent meetings in southern Illinois in the spring of 1908
- Marie Burgess preached in Chicago, Toledo, Detroit, and New York City. There, she founded Glad Tidings Hall (hub for the spreading Pentecostal revival)
- Another early Pentecostal pioneer in New York was Miss Maud Williams (Haycroft).

Canadian and European Pioneers of Pentecostalism

In Canada, some early pioneers of the Pentecostal movement included Ellen Hebden in Toronto, Ella M. Goff in Winnipeg, Alice B. Garrigus in Newfoundland, the Davis sisters in the Maritime provinces, Mrs. C. E. Baker in Montreal, and Zelma Argue throughout all of the Canadian provinces. Aimee Semple McPherson of Ingersoll, Ontario, began a preaching ministry in 1915 in Toronto that moved along the U.S. Eastern Seaboard, then westward across the United States in 1918. She eventually founded Angelus Temple in 1923, where she continued as senior pastor until her death in 1944.

An outstanding authoress and minister at the turn of the century was Jesse Penn-Lewis who was directly involved with the revival in Wales. Evan Roberts, the chief evangelist of the Welsh revival joined Mrs. Lewis in penning some of her writings on the overcoming life. Mrs. Lewis had a wide public ministry. Perhaps the most popular book she wrote was *War on the Saints,* a book on spiritual warfare.

Development of the Pentecostal Movement in the Twentieth Century

Kathryn Kuhlman's ministry began in the summer of 1923. After her ordination by the Evangelical Church Alliance in Joliet, Illinois, she established the Denver Revival Tabernacle in 1935, which she pastored for three years. In the mid-1940s, she went to Franklin, Pennsylvania, where she began to thrive as a preacher and radio evangelist. Many people were healed with notable miracles at her meetings beginning in 1947, and she gained a reputation as one of the outstanding healing evangelists, carrying on as a leading figure during the charismatic movement until her death in 1976.

Finally, permit me to mention other prominent women whose ministries flourished during the charismatic movement of the 1960s and 1970s: Baker, Myrtle D. Beall, Helen Beard, Aimee Cortese, Sue Curran, B. Maureen Gaglardi, Anne Giminez, Ione Glaeser, Hattie Hammond, Alpha A. Henson, Marilyn Hickey, Violet Kitely, Janet Kreis, Freda Lindsay, and Fuchsia T. Pickett. We should also include Iverna Tompkins, Rachel Titus, Eleanor and Roberta Armstrong, Rita Bennett, Edith Blumhofer, Hazel Bonawitz, Roxanne Brant, Mary Ann Brown, Shirley Carpenter, Jean Darnall, Josephine Massynberde Ford, Katie Fortune, Shirlee Green, Nina Harris, Sue Malachuk, Daisy Osborn, Dorothy Ranaghan, Agnes Sanford, Gwen Shaw, Bernice Smith, Ruth Carter Stapleton, Jean Stone, Joni Eareckson Tada, and Corrie Ten Boom. These women represent only a sampling of the important female figures that have been mightily used of God in every conceivable capacity of ministry leadership in the church throughout this period of church history.

Summary

As we demonstrated in Part Two that the Scriptures prove that women belong in ministry leadership, here, in Part Three, we see the record of Church History also bears ample testimony that as far as God is concerned, women belong in leadership. Now we turn to the ultimate question regarding women in leadership, *is God male or female?*

ENDNOTES

124 Tucker & Liefeld, 130.
125 Ibid. , 103.
126 Ibid. , 124.
127 Ibid. , 124.
128 John Chrysostom, *The Kind of Women Who Ought to Be Taken as Wives,* IV, quoted in Clark, *Women in the Early Church,* 37. Quoted in Tucker & Liefeld, 124.
129 Tucker & Liefeld, 91.
130 Ibid. , 90.
131 Elizabeth A. Clark, *Women in the Early Church. Message of the Fathers of the Church,* no. 13 (Wilmington: Glazier, 1983), 15. Quoted in Tucker & Liefeld, 90.
132 Tucker & Liefeld, 125.
133 John Chrysostom, *Homily 7 on Matthew,* 6. Quoted in Tucker & Liefeld, 125
134 Tucker & Liefeld, 125.
135 Durant, *Age of Faith,* 973. Quoted in Tucker & Liefeld, 164.
136 Ibid.
137 Tucker & Liefeld, 164.
138 Durant, *Age of Faith,* 973. Quoted in Tucker & Liefeld, 164-165.
139 Ibid.
140 Ibid. , 172.

PART FOUR

Chapter 10

Is Male Leadership Superior Because God Is Male?

I remember when the gender of God first occurred to me. I was driving and observed a bumper sticker that read: "Trust in God—She will provide." I can still recall my immediate sense that God was being diminished, even insulted.

I had always been aware that Jesus was of the masculine gender. Since I sang hymns that referred to God as "Father", "Lord", and "He", I assumed that my Heavenly Father also bore a masculine gender. So I dismissed the bumper sticker as a ploy of the radical feminist movement.

Then, as Detractors would confront me, I found them embracing the idea that since God is "Our Father" the masculine gender must be reserved for the top positions in the headship. I found them flirting with the idea that top spiritual leadership is a "male thing".

So, as I conclude this discussion on female and male leadership, I wanted to tackle one final question—does God in heaven assume a masculine identity? After all, the Bible does refer to God as a "He"; how about the 170 references to God as "Father"? How can one be a father unless he is male?

Then there is the matter of the Greek word for God, "*Theos,*" in the New Testament being a noun in the masculine case. My conclusion: God has chosen to relate to humankind via this identity even though, in terms of His true nature, God is not male.

Females in ministry leadership walk a very fine line. We still have our headship issues within our marriage relationship to respect and manage. We are bound by many cultural and Biblical factors. We derive spiritual empowerment by conducting ourselves in modesty. Yet, the modern world tends to interpret a genteel feminine demeanor as lacking in strength and fortitude, therefore, not the stuff of one who assumes a leadership role.

If you doubt this, think of those females in ministry leadership who bring to their pulpit presentations a very masculine, assertive bearing. In addition, we have all observed on the evening news, female leaders in the liberal mainline denominations who either embrace the lesbian lifestyle, or feel that assuming its persona is a form of empathy.

Combine that with a presumption that the Father and the Son are males, and you can see where my Detractors could jump to the conclusion that the female psyche lacks the emotional bearing required to lead men as a vocational minister.

On the other hand, take away the presumption of the Father and Son choosing a male on the assumption that it is better suited to lead ministries involving men, and we are forced to consider leadership without a gender bias. Leadership then becomes strictly a matter of the sovereign selection of God without regard for any gender preference.

Therefore, I dedicate this final discussion to this theological issue that will remove the last brickbat my Detractors felt they could throw at me—their last argument against women in leadership.

To help you appreciate the thinking of my Detractors I share the thinking of a pioneer in the Pentecostal movement, the author of the Annotated Reference Bible—Finis Dake. His conviction that God is male led him to describe God in this manner: "He (God) has a personal spirit body, shape, form, image and likeness of a man, bodily parts such as, back parts, heart, hands and fingers, mouth, lips and tongue, feet, eyes, hair, head, face, arms, loins, and other bodily parts. He has bodily presence and goes place to place in a body like all other persons. He has a voice and countenance. He wears clothes, eats, and dwells in a mansion in a city located on a material planet called heaven."

After reading these words, other verses came to mind in which God speaks about Himself: "Of the Rock Who bore you, you were unmindful; you forgot the God Who travailed in your birth." (Deut. 32:18). A man giving birth; how fascinating! Needless to say, I could produce a hundred verses that prove Rev. Dake's description of God as essentially male as nonsensical.

To hope to know of God's gender, or lack thereof, one will have to build the answer from factual evidence recorded in the Bible. After extensive investigation I have arrived at these vital facts that contribute toward the resolution of this question:

First, God is a Spirit, therefore does not possess human characteristics or limitations (John 4:24) and cannot be male in a physical form.

Second, God is a Person, therefore has all of the characteristics of personhood, including a mind, will, intellect and relationships. He also communicates, builds relationships, all of which are revealed in Scripture.

Third, because He is beyond human understanding, figurative language (called anthropomorphisms) is appropriate for finite minds to be able to understand something of His nature by comparing it to earthly similarities.

Next, while the English translation says that man and woman were created in God's image (Gen. 1:26-27), the Hebrew text says they were only patterned after His image, therefore not "carbon copies". This is important because it removes from God the necessity to possess male or female features since being made in His image has nothing to do with physical characteristics.

Then, one must consider this: gender's primary purpose is for sexual reproduction, which is a biological mechanism to allow DNA to recombine in different and potentially novel combinations. However, since our relationship with YHWH is spiritual, vs. physical, then the issue of gender becomes irrelevant.

Finally, one must realize that the Hebrew language does not label nouns and pronouns as masculine or feminine as we do in English. It does not even have a neuter case. Therefore, it never assigns a word as masculine or feminine based on its true nature, as we do in English. Let me explain.

Take the word "cow" in English. We know this is of the female gender of the bovine species. So we assign its noun a feminine "case" (grammatical identity). Likewise, the bull we label as "masculine". In addition, we think of a tree as a thing, therefore, assign it a neuter case.

Not so in Hebrew! It has no neuter case. So it labels the noun, "tree", as a masculine case. You could translate the phrase, "the tree was..." as "the tree (he) was..." . The decision was not based on any idea of sexuality, but rather was assigned as a purely grammatical decision (to enable a reader to identify the nouns with their modifier pronouns). As a result, the noun, "tree", happens to have masculine case endings without any regard for its true gender. None!

That being the case, does that mean that all those hundreds of references to God as "He" has nothing to do with Him being male? You learn fast.

This Hebrew structure is so helpful, because it frees God to be both a Father to the fatherless, and a Mother to those hurting and in pain. He can assume any gender identity because He, being pure Spirit, has none.

So What

In light of all these facts, what can we know about the gender of God? This composite conclusion emerges: since God is a single unborn, uncreated being, He is also a non-biological entity. He is a Spirit which has no body, therefore, is beyond the need for, or capacity for any gender-based identity. Also, any reference in the Old Testament to God as "He" should not be construed as having any reference to gender.

And what might we conclude from this composite body of information about gender and leadership? His selection in calling a man or woman for ministry leadership will be based on His sovereign will and not on gender considerations.

True, the Scriptures do refer to God hundreds of times with masculine names and with masculine pronouns such as "he," "him," and "his", and never uses feminine pronouns such as "she," her," and "hers." Is this usage purely generic, such as our use of "man" to refer to both men and women? Or is there a deeper reason?

I believe there is. Considering the options, thinking of God as male makes good theological, and philosophical sense. Let's explore the alternatives to appreciate the special use of the masculine pronoun.

God as "It"

I shudder at the idea of considering the pronoun to modify the noun "God" as an "it", because it would reduce God from a sovereign Being apart from creation to a force existing within the ongoing realm of creation. We then are faced with the fact that the polytheistic religions based on the Eternal force, and the innocuous sense of Being are all that the human heart has to turn to for hope. I would not want to minister or even live in such a world left to animal instincts to find meaning in life.

If God were an "it", Christianity and Judaism would be reduced to polytheism, or animism or any of the thousands of varieties of religions based on the eternal idea, or whatever (it has many names).

God as "She"

Again, this pronoun would elevate the evil cults that Paul faced in Ephesus and Corinth as well as the multitude of religions in Africa and Latin America to the threshold of legitimacy. Surely this is unthinkable, especially in light of the essential moral values we know to be essential to civilization that would be impugned by people racing to church for sexual favors, or blood sacrifice of children, or any of a multitude of atrocities all designed to appease some concocted deity so that the crops might grow into a prosperous harvest, or the wombs of its mothers bear children.

If my study of religion has taught me anything it is that this concept of "theacrocy"—the embracing of the eternal "She" –has unleashed more cruelty on the unborn, as well as women and children in general. No thank you, I would not want to live in a society that thinks of God as primarily concerned with a perennially bad disposition appeased by evil and sin perpetrated at the highest level of government and religion for life to have ongoing existence.

The other reason I oppose the use of the feminine pronoun (she) is that it fails to protect an attribute of God, namely His transcendence from the illusion, espoused by paganism, that nature is born from God as a mother rather than created. Recall that the Ephesian cult actually believed that Adam was born of Eve since the source of all life is the woman as the eternal mother. By referring to Him as a "He", sex based cults are eliminated. Remember, if God were a "she" then the religions that Paul battled in Ephesus and Corinth would have credibility.

No, I much prefer to think of God as "He", and for the theological and philosophical safeguards. In this context five reasons come to mind.

Sovereignty

As I have shown, while God intended both men and women to share leadership in the building of His kingdom, He ordained that they approach leadership according to their own inherent natures, and therefore differently. Women are nurturers, the glue that holds spiritual organizations together from within. Male leadership sets boundaries and acts entrepreneurially. As such it is very good at deciding structure, i.e., defining the healthy organization by the establishment of rules. Men are better at this, in my opinion than women. That is not to say that female leadership is not capable of establishing moral, ethical, and organizational boundaries. I am saying, I feel they are naturally better at this function.

There is a special role in the leadership group for one who assumes the role as "sovereign". People seemed surprised when I say this because they think that being a woman called to leadership means that I do not require the role of "sovereign" to partner with—i.e., that I am the sovereign. No, in my ministry I am required to shoulder much responsibility. But in the overall direction of our congregation, I defer to a Board in which I participate with other people, both male and female. I consider this Board my sovereign guide.

Therefore, I do see the necessity for someone in leadership to assume ultimate sovereign leadership, and in the Godhead, this falls to the Father. So, calling God "He" perfectly describes the masculine side of God's leadership.

There is also another reason I feel the use of the masculine pronoun to modify the noun "God": It provides a "natural" reason for obedience. In the family, the father's role is the one all defer to in rendering obedience. Therefore, it is natural for God to be referred to as a "He" in order to facilitate obedience.

The third reason for using the masculine pronoun in reference to God is that it moves the work of salvation out of the reach of being thought of as something achieved by God and man working in a partnership.

The fourth reason for considering God as male is that it enables us to use the human family with its essential gender distinctions to be a useful metaphor for the infinitely complex relationship between the members of the Godhead and their respective roles in accomplishing their ultimate purpose for creation.

Like fatherhood precedes the birth of children, so salvation begins in the mind of the Father and is accomplished by the Son. Therefore, it remains for the children to embrace it as their hope for eternal life by repentance and faith. "He" is the eternal Father, therefore, salvation is His doing; and ours is to respond or reject it as our hope.

Immanence

The fifth benefit of referring to God as "He" is that it also spares the Biblical revelation about God from becoming polytheistic, with a vast number of gods and goddesses clamoring for worship. God as a "He" can get very close to the human condition since He is apart from our world, yet able to move closely to provide help.

In addition to these theological reasons, permit me to add one final important reason. We refer to God as "He" because the Divine Author of the Scriptures chose to use the pronoun in reference to Himself. In this, my thoughts return to the words of Isaiah: "Shall the clay say to the Potter?"

So I am very comfortable referring to God as "He", especially since I know that it provides my Detractors with an occasion to think that male leadership is superior because it is more like the nature of God.

Summary

So, if any of you Detractors who have dogged my ministry for two decades think you can take comfort in the fact that because the English Bible speaks of God using the masculine pronoun or Case then, He prefers male ministry leaders as a sort of "guy thing", sorry. C'mon now, you can no longer use that one in making an intelligent defense of your position.

You can place such contrived ideas in that pile where you had to toss your arguments that you felt the four key New Testament verses proved women do not belong in ministry leadership.

Yes, toss it alongside that pile where you were forced to discard your notions about the Bible and church history supporting your fallacious thesis that God does not call women into ministry leadership.

Do not fear, not all is lost. One tenable position remains.

True, it will not be easy to embrace; but, then isn't that where the masculine gender shines—being strong, doing the hard thing?

So brace yourself, rear back on your hind legs, and receive this stark truth like, well, like a man.

I will reduce it to a simple axiom you can ingest without choking…

…Women do belong in ministry leadership!